BLAXHAUSTION, KARENS & OTHER THREATS TO BLACK LIVES AND WELL-BEING

A Black Woman's Perspective

THERESA M. ROBINSON

Master Trainer TMR & Associates, LLC

Master Trainer TMR & Associates, LLC
Houston, TX
+1.346.800.2822
info@MasterTrainerTMR.com

Theresa M. Robinson, author

ISBN 978-0-9988420-8-0 Paperback

First Edition

This is a work of nonfiction. Some names and identifying details have been changed.

Credits:
Editor Erika Winston, Personal Touch Edits, Washington, DC
Cover Designer Maria Stoian, 99Designs
Interior Designer Mark Robinson, Master Trainer TMR & Assoc., Houston, TX

Dedication

To The Source of all living things Who makes all things possible.

    To my mum, who gave me safe passage.

    To Mark, Baylie, Max, and JoAnn whose love and support are a cherished respite from the Blaxhaustion.

    To my Black sisters in the daily struggle—
I see you.
I hear you.
I am you.

Table of Contents

Foreword Fire!   i

Acknowledgments   vii

Introduction   1

Act I: Blaxhaustion™   45

Act II: Karens, Her Ken, and Her Kin   81

Act III: Coronaviracism™: A Tale of Two Pandemics   129

Act IV: Great White Lies   157

Act V: White Complicity & Performative Wokeness   191

Conclusion   237

Oppression Dictionary   251

About the Author   259

Other Books by Author   261

Connect with Author   263

Foreword Fire!

Denise Branch

Denise Branch here, and I'm speaking. Yes, Mr. & Mrs. Anti-Black Racism, I'm speaking because "the sexist of my racist is my sexist and my racist" and I'm fucking suffering from blaxhaustion. Black women's intersectional experiences don't matter to Amerikkka, Karen, Ken, and any of you! Aren't Black women, women too? America, Black women just saved you. If American feminism isn't intersectional and anti-racist too, is American feminism only for Karen, Amy, Becky, and assimilation but not #metoo? Tell the truth!

I am blaxhausted from all of the white lies, aren't you? Whiteness must become learners, and whiteness from a different color mustn't uphold liars. As Kimberly Crenshaw, a Black woman leading scholar of critical race theory who developed the theory of intersectionality says, the urgency of intersectional feminism is now. It is harmful towards Black women to continue to ignore intersectionality. America's war on Black women allows you not to hear her color or her pain because you want to continue to harm her. Why, I wonder do Black women warrant such anti-Black hate? What do Black women represent that is such a threat?

In *Blaxhaustion, Karens & Other Threats to Black Lives and well-Being*, author Theresa M. Robinson has brought together a provocative anthology of Black women truth-tellers, mic-droppers, fire-speakers from across the globe who are each speaking up and giving zero fucks! Everybody else can just shut the fuck up and listen. On these pages, are the truths about the America we live in. Read between their womanist lines that cut across anti-Black racist minds. Black women are no longer being silent about the anti-Black hate and the Karens, Kens, and their Kin or anyone aligning with them.

Silence will not save us from the anti-Black racism that we face from every race. We can't end racism until we end anti-Black racism. Silence will not save us from the anti-Black racism that threatens our lives and well-being in the workplace and the world-place. Anti-Blackness anywhere threatens Blackness everywhere. The racial terrorism and the systemic racism faced by Black people across the world daily are blaxhausting. We're no longer going to pay the price for your anti-Black racism in the workplace or world-place. Our lives are priceless.

Racism is a pandemic! The American Medical Association just recognized racism as a public health threat. So that Black lives can be saved, where is the vaccine for racists?

Anti-Blackness continues to show its ugly face within white feminism. White feminism sold us out in 2016, and it sold us out again in 2020 (and during the suffragette movement). White feminist racism is real. I'm a womanist. To me, it doesn't make sense now to be anything else after the election. I'm not going to play feminist games with white women whose actions are a daily threat to the lives and well-being of their same gender and to the Black community at large. Clearly racism kills, and two-faced white feminism has no interest in fighting to end the deadly racism that kills Black women who look like the women speaking out in the pages of this book.

You cannot be both at once a feminist and racist. Choose one! After the senseless murders of George Floyd and Breonna Taylor, along with those that preceded them and those that came after them, Black women were not okay. Also Black men were not okay, and Black children were not okay. But white women thought it was okay to vote again for anti-Black racism. In fact, white women continue to bring up sexism, sexism,

sexism over our dead bodies while we're in the middle of a life-and-death racial struggle at the hands of their racist husbands, fathers, sons, uncles, nephews and beyond.

Death by racism was not a dealbreaker for white women at the polls. White women don't see Black women and girls lives as worthy of fighting for and saving in the name of feminism. Thus it is safe to say most white women are white men in heels. White women are the key to white supremacy's continued success.

History also reminds me that our Black women ancestors were once white women's property, and that is why their descendants don't see Black women as their equals. White women hold a unique position and privilege in society as both one of the oppressed and one of the oppressors. We can't allow Jim Crow's daughters and grand-daughters to keep flying under the radar under the guise of being allies and women, too.

Through viral video, white women have proven to be a danger to the lives and well-being of Black men, women, and children even during a deadly pandemic. White women can be found in all facets of anti-Black racism in American history and have been white supremacy's most loyal foot soldiers in heels long before we had the technology to capture them on video. They have been the reason for thousands, if not millions, of murdered Black people, especially Black men and Black boys.

Fighting anti-Black racism is like breathing to me. I'm not tired of breathing. I'm going to continue fighting on the front lines of racist minds for my community to breathe racism-free air. It's part of how we will survive. We can't breathe without it.

The Black community should no longer have to feel the "threat" of everyday anti-Black racism. It's been a blaxhausting four years for Black people. Anytime "good" white people and so-called allies see a threat to Black lives, they can start putting their mouths and bodies in between Black people and racists.

Black women are facing overwhelming blaxhaustion from being on the front lines fighting white supremacy, while too many others haven't put their gloves on because they're in bed with white supremacy. When will Black men replace Black women on the front lines? When can Black women take the gloves off to rest? Every Black man must stand up, speak up, and join the fight.

From Harriet Tubman fighting to free us from chains to Stacey Abrams fighting to keep us from going back in chains, Black women have been mainly a stand-alone army against white men and white supremacy at large. We have been the fighters, our own cut women, corner women, promoters, trainers, coaches, mentors, hype women.

Black women are fucking exhausted from trying to save Black men and boys from dying—and we've been doing it without undying support. If you came from a Black woman, how can you not be in the fight to protect them? Black women know *we can't win the fight* to protect the well-being and save the lives of all in the Black community *if we're not in the fight* to protect the well-being and save the lives of all in the Black community. The 21st century has shown us that if not Black women, then who?

May the truth of our words sting like a bee. The Black community should not still be feeling the sting of 1960's anti-Black racism in 2020. Black women have always been truth-tellers for the world.

Theresa has written a masterpiece with the invaluable support of Black women who don't give a DAYUUMMM about white feelings or the feelings of whiteness from a different color, but do give a damn about ending the blaxhaustion, Karens and other threats to Black Lives and well-being. We said what we said. We wrote what we wrote! Don't call us angry. Call us truth-tellers. Call us passionate about saving Black lives and livelihoods, especially after fighting anti-Black racism, white feminism, and white supremacy every day! Whew, America, fuck y'all anti-Black racism! Fuck y'all white feminism! Fuck y'all white supremacy! I'm tired of it fucking with me! Denise Branch here, and I've spoken.

Denise Branch is an anti-racism educator, consultant, coach, and speaker who was named by Forbes as one of "7 Anti-Racism Educators Your Company Needs Now." Referred to as the MLK of DEI by her professional DEI peers, Denise is highly sought out for her expertise in developing anti-racist employers and employees. Her life's work has been on the front lines of the racism pandemic changing racist minds to save Black lives and Black livelihoods. In addition to developing anti-racist people, Denise also serves as a trusted advisor to organizations who seek her out to develop anti-racist programming, partnerships, purchasing, phil-anthropy, policies, and practices.

Acknowledgments

Mark Robinson, my life partner and business partner, my general manager, my book project manager, my agent, and my bodyguard, who knows me better than anyone and who pushes me harder and greater than anyone. For all the reasons that matter, I remain smitten and eternally grateful after a 30-year partnership.

Denise Branch, sistahQueen, auntie, and one of the original voices of anti-Black racism speaking out when there was great risk in doing so. Continuously blazing new trails and sharing powerful truths, she is the standard to which few can compare. With a fire and wit that are legendary, she has my tribute and respect both inside and outside of these pages.

Dr. Kimya Nuru Dennis, sistahQueen, my "Just Us Pajama Party" (JUPP) series partner, and also one of the original voices of anti-Black racism. Her intense passion for fighting injustice makes her a giant in all spaces. She stands strong in her convictions, and I honor her unwavering spirit.

Teddi Williams, sistahQueen and inspiration, who early on planted a vision seed that stayed with me. She embodies the strength of the ancestors. The lyrical and ancestral power of her poetry gives this book a deeply spiritual resonance that culminates in a beautiful "call-and-response" that honors and summons to the stage 62 sistahQueen voices.

Erika Winston, sistahQueen and my miracle-worker editor, who embraced and believed in this project and whose shared lived experiences and expertise helped immensely in guiding, shaping, and elevating my raw, unfiltered words. My deepest gratitude is not enough.

Sixty-two "I'm Speaking" sistahQueen contributors, who, each in Black sisterhood and solidarity, raise their voices in testimony to unique lived experiences arising from the Black diaspora.

Alana M. Hill

Alisha C. Gray

Ashley McGirt

Baylie Robinson

CaJuana Capps

Cassandra Binkley

Chris Wright

Dr. Danyelle Wright

DeAnnah Stinson Reese

Debbie Holmes

Dee Perry

Deloria Nelson Streete

Dianna Parker

Dianne Greyson

Emeline Mugisha

Ericka S. Riggs

Erika M. Di Renzo

Erin Jones

Etta Jacques Jones

Future Cain

Huldah Akita

Janeisha Cambridge

Janelle Benjamin

Dr. Janice Gassam Asare

JeNae Johnson

Jo Bonsell

Joelle A. Murchison

Jonee Meiser

Keyonna A. Monroe

Kimberly Jones

Lakesha Mathis

Leah Slater-Radway

LeNeice Gavin

Lisa Hurley

Lynne Stokes

Michelle McFarland-McDaniels

Monique Braham-Evans

Rachel Rudo Munyaradzi

Ruth Elizabeth Chale Pepito

Dr. Sarah Blair-Reid

Sedruola Maruska

Sharla Stevens

Sharon Hurley Hall

Shelly-Ann Wilson Henry

Dr. Shindale Seale

Shirley Ebikebina Moser-Onduru

Sibyl Biggers

Simone Wright

Sommer Sibilly-Brown

Sophia J. Casey

Dr. Susan Jenkins

Tameca Miles

Dr. Tammy L. Hodo

Tanesha Kelly

Taye Johnson

Teeona Mayberry

Themum Crawford

Thordis Howard

Tiana Conley

Tiffany Salmon

Vanessa Womack

Venita Stewart-Wilson

Introduction

Chief (A Poem)

Chief

Chief-Daughter

Chief-Sistah

Chief-Mother

Chief as you walk down the street

Chief as you stop

Then speak

Chief when someone was in trouble

Chief hurry hurry on the double

To save the maimed

To give to the poor others abhor

Providing warmth to the cold and shelter to so many of those without

Help
Love
A voice
A choice

[A] Woman can be [a] Chief, too
Hmph Hmph Hmph

If only they knew

You gave and you gave

Never

To

Cave

In

You give and you give

Only to win

Your chocolate of skin
Their rarest of our kin
Beau-ti-ful

Yes!

Resembles a black pearl
Hell, Mama we're just squirrels trying to keep space in your
world

When you say what you say and said what you said and speak
what you speak

To sit now at your feet

It's more than a treat, in fact—it's treasure

Rarer and more rarer

It isn't everyday children, young and old in a world that can
be so so cold, frigid and rigid

Have an opportunity to hear you speak

When we are tired you speak
Into us what was taken from us
When we are able you speak stable
Into us
When we frown it is you Chief that looks down bringing us
Back
Up
Encouraging us All...never ever give up

Chief-Daughter

Chief-Sistah

Chief-Mother

Chief as you walk down the street

Chief as you stop

Then speak

The words you speak
Let us know
all
we de-siiiiire
Yes!

Is within reach

— Teddi Williams

5

I wrote what I wrote

Theresa M. Robinson here, and I'm speaking. What lies ahead in these pages defies conformity and seeks not one iota of approval from whiteness, nor does it rely on the use of white conventions, forms, or protocols. In other words, language rules and writing conventions be damned. My damn book. My damn rules.

If I end up citing something, I'll cite it in a manner of my choosing without adherence to formal footnote formatting rules. I cannot care less about MLA, APA, or CMS styles when Black people are suffering and dying all around me. If there is no source cited, that means I. Am. The. Source.

Me, Theresa.

Black woman.

Black wife.

Black mother.

Black daughter.

Black sister.

Black friend. (unless you're white and tout me as "your one Black friend," then NO, I'm NOT your friend)

These are my thoughts, my views, my knowledge, my experiences culminating from 50+ years of living while Black.

My entire life.

In short, me and Black women been writin' this our WHOLE life. And yes, I know that sentence doesn't reflect standard "proper" English, but it's my set-up for the warning I'm about to drop.

Warning. I almost don't wanna include a warning statement with this book, but I know that at least two groups of malintentioned women[1]— (1) nosey undercover Karens and (2) sell-out Candaces—will pick up this book to slam it, me, and the voices of the Black women it features and honors. Make no mistake. This is a heads-up and not an apology. My words will not be veiled in political correctness, tactfulness, civility, or etiquette or any of that other muzzling white supremacy nonsense.

For MY comfort – did you get that? – MY comfort, I'll be using a variety of mixed languages and expressions, code-switches, and Black "virtue-signaling" that reflect a lifetime of navigating and mastering white spaces and language while staying true to my eastside J'ville roots. I'm one of "the Mathis sisters" from Duval county Florida where we swept the dirt back from the stretch of street in front of our house and looked to the streetlights as our curfew clock.

In other words, I'ma be talkn' bout and sayin' all kinda stuff in ways that I think it, see it, feel it, and live it. Past tense and present tense. Don't nobody wanna be all the time self-editing and self-adjusting for somebody else's comfort. Nah. Not today. This book ain't about elevating the colonizer's language, language rules, or language etiquette. This book ain't about glorifying whiteness or white spaces. Hell, it ain't even about trying to gain access to white spaces. Beyond already showing white folks—as if I shoulda ever needed to—that I'm "white people smart," I ain't got nothing to "prove." Karen and Candace'nem can hit bricks.

If you get offended and lose your shit at the mere suggestion of an off-color (pun intended) insight or an experience,

---

[1] Though my warning explicitly calls out white women and BIPOC women who value proximity to whiteness, this warning also applies to anyone who actively or passively engages in marginalization, character assassination, or dehumanization of Black women.

then too bad, boo-hoo, and cry me a river. This book ain't for you no way. Don't let the back cover hit you on yo' way out.

If you're quick to claim that I'm hating on and "bashing" white folks or stoking division, you can keep it moving. Yeah, I will be speaking against the racist social construct of whiteness and the archetypes – white or otherwise – that embrace whiteness and deny Black humanity. And if I sometimes conflate whiteness with white people, oh well...deal with it. It's an understandable "mistake." You might suffer a hurt feeling or two, buttercup, but nothing like the feeling of getting shot while existing.

Before you decide to rage against me, my sisters, or this book, make sure you acknowledge that you stepped into an explicitly identified space and tried to impose those very same decentering and silencing tactics that I'm writing about.

So go ahead...huff and puff, clutch your pearls, toss back your hair, turn up your nose in the air of your own stench, and call me every name I've already been called before.

I am still here.

I will still be here.

I wrote what I wrote.

Girl, bye.

A Word About "Not All..."

We've all been privy to "not all white people" and "not all white women" in response to our experiences. Yes, not all white people are actively racist. Yes, not all white women are Karens. Guess what? I'ma need us to take a spoon full of our own medicine so that we recognize that it's also "not all Black people" and "not all Black men" and "not all Black women" in response to our experiences with tompromised™ folks, sell-out folks, and Candaces. I'ma be dropping my thoughts on both foul whiteness and foul Blackness. That's right. Foul

Blackness. Not all skinfolk are kinfolk, and they also prove a threat to our lives and well-being. See what I just did there? *Not all* skinfolk are kinfolk. We can't pick and choose when we want this to be conveniently true.

Please spare me the righteous indignation. I look forward to hearing about it when you write *your* book. Ain't nobody got time to be catering to and anticipating Black sensitivity and Black defensiveness when it's time for us to confront our own stuff. So tailor the narrative however you need to with an implicit "some" or "most" or "all" that works for you and the triggered nerve you need to quell. Cuz still... I wrote what I wrote.

They Came for Me

Whew, chile! The "blacklash" was swift and harsh. White folks showed out and completely. Lost. Their. Shit.

My offense?

I had "dared" to share on LinkedIn, a "professional" social media platform, my microaggression experience from a December 2019 flight on Delta airlines.

From there, all white hell broke loose. Karens, and Beckys, and Kens, and Brads—all of them—spilled out of the woodwork like cockroaches do when the light turns on. They came at me hard over a 1200-character count narrative about my experience.

Racism and white supremacy don't take a single day off – ever. (Look around. Racism is baked into every day. White supremacy is baked into every day.)

And, to top it off, a few Black men pulled up with that "you-shoulda-listened-to-your-husband" patriarchy crap. Don't get me wrong. I love myself some Black men, but they can be such asses. Though they are not as bad as white women who choose whiteness over gender, the Black men we love as brothers, boyfriends, or husbands can get caught up in that dominance mess. Hmph. They better call Tyrone cuz I am not the one.

Anyhoo, between the white folks with their racism and the Black men with their patriarchal condescension, my narrative blew up with over 100K views in a matter of days. While most of the comments were supportive and empathetic, many were vicious.

Really? Seriously? You'da thought I was relaying how I had hijacked the plane or something based on how fast and furious whiteness and patriarchy had come for me.

Here, word-for-word, is what set them off.

So this happened yesterday on Delta Air Lines. I and a white guy behind me boarded the plane carrying our coats. Flight attendant looks past me and assumes he's in first class and offers to take his coat until he tells her he's in 11C.

So I turn back to her and say, "I'm in 4D. Will you take mine?" Guess it didn't occur to her to assume I'm in first class.

When I shared this with hubby, he sent me a text. Hope our unedited texting provides insight to non-POC on why POC are sick, why POC are tired, why POC are sick-and-tired.

Hubby to me— "If you're in the mood and it's appropriate and you have the privacy to do it, it would be informative to discuss what happened with the flight attendant and get her perception and share your perception with her. And it's not even like you're dressed casually today."

Me to hubby— "Don't have the bandwidth to deal with it right now. That's part of the impact of microaggressions that people of color deal with. Some days we are just too exhausted from the same shit over and over to address each and every instance. I am in full business attire—suit with jacket. Now imagine if I had on jeans and my Skechers that I traveled in yesterday. Again, this kinda stuff wears on folks. It's death by a thousand cuts."

This account of my experience, which included the transcript of the text exchange between me and my husband, is what unleashed the rage.

I had crossed one of the visibly invisible lines of whiteness, one of the understood rules of white supremacy—I should never ever talk about, highlight, or "complain" about my own oppression within hearing distance of the oppressors. They don't like it. It makes them uneasy and uncomfortable. It compels them to make an example out of me.

With consequences that were immediate and ongoing, I was punished by whiteness for several months afterwards because I dared to bring attention to a racial microaggression. Let's see. I was called racist and sexist.

I was accused of playing the race card.

I was diagnosed as having a victim mentality.

I was slammed for being full of hate.

I was accused of having a chip on my shoulder.

Additionally, my experience was discounted and dismissed as "crap" and "a contrived piece of baloney." Those aren't even the worst things leveled at me, but I'm choosing to not give misogynoir a voice here.

The pattern of hate was quite interesting though. The aggressive attacks mostly originated with insecure white men suffering from small-dick energy. And the nice-nasty passive-aggressive comments mostly came from white women who …well, ya know…who are…just so…extra.

Clearly there was nothing "micro" about any of this for me—neither the microaggression itself nor the mere sharing of it. And it's never just the one—neither the microaggression nor the racist asshole that gets triggered if you talk about it.

They rarely occur in isolation.

They travel in packs.

They feed off each other.

Okay. Enough for now about the assholes. Let me get laser-focused on racial microaggressions for a moment.

Racial microaggressions are best characterized as the everyday racism that we face in the form of "compliments," jokes, insults, and just plain ole' ignorance. For the record, I hate the term microaggression and would prefer something more accurate such as "regularly occurring racist bullshit" or the "stupid shit white folks say," but for the sake of efficiency, I'll go with microaggression for now.

Consider for a moment that we're born frogs in the water, and over our lifetime we've lived in water with a temperature that has steadily risen to boiling.

Not everybody's water heats up and boils like ours.

Not everybody's water is polluted like ours.

Not everybody's water is used as a dumping site for every-body else's crap.

No. Not even non-Black POCs live in water like ours.

And when we're physically, emotionally, and mentally troubled or sick at disproportionately higher rates, no one looks at the huge contributing factor of the water. Instead, they continue to think that something must be inherently wrong with the frog. And so they advise the frog—that lives in the dirty boiling water that THEY made dirty and boiling—to stop with all the croaking and just pull itself up by its webbed feet.

Racism in all of its manifestations ultimately makes us sick and kills us prematurely. The stress of racism is undeniable. I don't need a "white" paper or a white-sanctioned research study to point it out. I just know. We just know. And there is not a white person on this planet who would willingly trade places with us knowing what we face. Jane Elliott already had that meeting with them, and they agreed.

One of the many stressors of racism involves being on the receiving end of the "what's the big deal?" gaslighting sentiment prevalent among the traffickers of microaggressions. I've never heard a single target of microaggressions characterize them as "not a big deal" or otherwise inconsequential. Not a single one.

I suppose it wouldn't be a big deal if we told a white woman that "she's pretty for a white girl."

I suppose it wouldn't be a big deal if we said to a white person, "You should meet my friend Ann. She's white, too!'

I suppose it wouldn't be a big deal if we said to a white man, "I won't be able to remember you name, so I'll call you Jamar."

If they could only imagine what it's like to hear that shit over and over and over again everywhere they go, for every space they inhabit. And then if they could imagine the tremendous energy required to resist the urge to open up a can of verbal whup-ass.

I suppose it also wouldn't be a big deal if I told a white man that "he doesn't sound white."

As a professional speaker and facilitator who frequently addresses all-white groups, I get to be on the receiving end of that microaggression all the time. It gets me every time—the "you're so articulate" pseudo-compliment. They honestly believe it's a compliment versus a betrayal of their belief that we are less competent coupled with a betrayal of their surprise that we are MORE than competent.

Even after nearly 30 years of hearing it, I continue to feel it like it's the first time each time. Though I can say that I'm used to HEARING it, I'm nowhere near used to FEELING it. My heart rate usually quickens while I try to control my facial expression and maintain "professionalism," all while preventing a middle-finger reflex.

"You're so articulate."

"I can't believe you were able to remain so articulate the whole time." (after a one-day training course)

"Great session. You didn't use a single 'um."

"You speak so *good*."

That last one provides me a bit of smug satisfaction in knowing that it violates one of *their* rules of proper English. The ability to speak and write English is one of the standards that whiteness uses to judge the intelligence of others.

These same judgers trash every aspect of our multi-lingualism and our ability to code-switch our way through colonizer language. These same judgers ridicule our artistry of the verb "to be." These same judgers hang grammatically-incorrect public signage that reads "10 items or less." Ha! The proper form is "10 items or fewer."[2]

---

[2] At times, I'll be serving up my perspective with a side-dish of petty not petty. Call it a side-effect of holding stuff in for so long and

Yeah, the same-ole' same-ole' microaggressions contribute greatly to blaxhaustion. These same old slights stemming from ignorant whiteness epitomize blaxhaustion.

I guess when they realized that there's nothing particularly special or standout-ish about whiteness, the entire construct of race—false superiority claims that depend on racial othering—makes complete sense for what it is. A cloak for mediocrity that seeks to grab and maintain power. The playbook basics have not changed; rather, the playbook is being constantly updated in real time.

Microaggressions have a sinister purpose to remind us of our station in society as "others." Why do I say this? Because I find it inconceivable that grown-ass people don't have the sense their momma gave 'em and don't know better than to ask to touch our hair! And because there has been so much spoken and written about this one—the "strangest" micro-aggression of them all—I'm convinced that they know exactly what they're doing when they ask. I'm also convinced that THE only appropriate response to this asinine request is a blunt force, "Hell naw, you can't touch my hair! What the actual fuck is wrong with you?!"

This Is Me

The me of all the worlds and spaces I've come to navigate comes with a multiplicity of complexities and nuances born of how I view myself and how the world views me. I have been conditioned to see me in all the ways I am seen and to prioritize that over how I see me.

---

having so much of my life dictated by the system of white supremacy. So for the white folks who stuck around after reading the warning, my words should prove quite tame in comparison to 4 years of the racist, misogynist, hate-mongering occupant in the big house.

If you want the full "girlfriend experience" so that you can know the me in these pages, then keep reading. It's here in this scene you'll discover my past that has brought me to where I am now. You will have a better sense of my journey which has led me to think and feel the way that I do. And though not every Black woman will relate to every single experience, I want you to walk away, sister, honoring my experience the way I honor yours.

If you are not looking for the full "girlfriend experience," go ahead and skip to the next scene, "Blaxhaustion Is a Real Thing."

Deep breath.

Okay. Now that I've cleared the earlier mal-intents from our space, and ushered ahead the rest, I want you who remains here with me to see me, sister. Really see me. All of me. Many of us have been so conditioned to blend in with whiteness for our survival that we've blocked us from really seeing us. We've also been blocked from seeing ourselves.

This is me. My name is Theresa Marie Mathis Robinson. Having navigated Blackness and whiteness all my life, I'm "fluent" in both. I speak the Queen's English, proper English, standard southern English, ivy league, HBCU, Blackety-Black, "just us," uppity Black, Black girlfriend, "niggah, pleez," side-eye, and "bitch, I will cutchu." I am all of these and more.

This is me. From my childhood, I know about a brand of domestic abuse tied to the powerlessness that my dad felt when constantly subjected to the "less-than" othering and the psychological beat-downs at the hands of white folks who minimized and symbolically castrated him—not with just the word "nigger," but also with the word "boy," which, by the way, cops still frequently use today. Both words carry a historical heaviness and a historical trauma with distinctly different and devastating impacts.

16

I lived in and witnessed the intermittent domestic abuse of my mum by my dad until I was 7 years old. That's when my mum finally had enough and kicked him out of the house, but not for that reason. For another "last straw" reason involving my dad's inability to grasp the basic concept that his wife and lover aren't supposed to be two separate women.

My dad—not able to cope with the cruel duality of imposed powerlessness coupled with the weight of being a husband, father, and provider—took out his frustration physically on my mum. True to her southern roots, my mum would signal a warning to my dad by putting a pot of boiling grits on the stove. Hot grits in my house were not always for eating. My mum, like other Black women at that time, were all too familiar with the fate of R&B singer Al Green whose ex-girlfriend had poured a pot of scalding-hot grits on him. Black men knew about the grits, too, and so my mum's tactic worked. My dad would see the pot on the stove and instead of startin' some mess, he'd just leave the house and stay gone for days.

As a Black woman, my mum was not guaranteed protection from anybody – not from white folks, not from Black men, not even from her husband. Much like Black women today, she had to fend for herself against even her own.

Retrospectively, I imagine she avoided getting hit many times simply by boiling those grits. But I don't know for sure because there are certain things we just don't talk about in my family. There are traumas too deep to bring up. To this day, eleven years after my dad's passing, my mum still doesn't broach the topic of her married life with my dad.

A sharecropper's son, my dad as a young kid was forced to drop out of the 3rd grade to financially help his parents. Field labor was backbreaking and yet despite the circumstances, he continued to teach himself. One of the shrewdest businessmen I know, he achieved financial success in his later years, and yet, like many of us, he held unresolved racial trauma. He likely died with it untreated and unresolved.

This is me. As a kid growing up, I was both gifted and Black. No. Not a brag. I legit earned the label. This combination of "gifted and Black" more than anything else in my life has profoundly shaped me and my identity.

At the urging of my first-grade teacher, my mum had me tested. I failed. (She should've had me tested for autism then, too. More about that later.) Five years later, she had me tested again. This time I passed. It wasn't until 8th grade though that I was enrolled in gifted classes.

For junior high school (which was 8th and 9th grade at that time), I was bussed to a predominantly white school where I was placed in gifted classes as "the only." Thus began my split identity crisis and consciousness. Regarded as a curiosity and a spectacle by teachers and white kids, I retreated even further into a world of books and writing that I had created for myself years earlier. It was during these years that I bought into the lie that I was shy. Shyness was not the reason that I didn't speak in my classes. I didn't speak because they didn't see me. I was invisible to them. I was ostracized and marginalized. And so I "learned" to be invisible. I learned to not speak up or speak out.

I gave them what they wanted, what they expected – classmates and teachers alike. I was a not-seen and not-heard version of me. When I knew the answers, I'd refrain from raising my hand. And if teachers called on me, I'd opt for, "I don't know" rather than take on the spotlight of scrutiny.

Years later in high school, I grew into even more of a curiosity as my white classmates often wondered and were amazed, for example, at how "the dumb, quiet little Black girl" (or so they thought) managed to pull an A from AP Calculus. You know how they do. They think there is some rift in the universe or a shift in the natural order when confronted with excellence that doesn't come packaged in a white wrapper. I lived for report card day just to see them step outside of the usual and ask me what grade I got. They probably thought somebody had rigged all the report cards. Because that's what entitled whiteness does when it realizes it isn't the best at something. Ha!

I was so good about listening to and observing the white kids. Because I was invisible, they would say and do stuff around me without giving it a second thought. The whole time I was learning and mastering how whiteness works. Unbeknownst to me at the time, I was also mastering how to appear neurotypical.

I spent more time around white kids at school than I did with Black kids because they were the ones in my classes. I had very few Black friends at school. Most thought I was "trying to be white" and steered clear of me. How I processed this and the dislocation of my identity stemmed from my feeling stuck—rejected by the white kids and not feeling accepted by the Black kids. Kinda like "racial limbo." I experienced most of my high school education as "the only." A fact that just is. I am neither proud nor ashamed.

During my last year of high school, which is supposed to be a special year, I was "immortalized" in the yearbook with a picture of me walking down the corridor with the caption, "Outstanding Negro Student." I was mortified and utterly devastated. It was a back-handed slight under the guise of a compliment – what today is termed—yup, you guessed it—a microaggression. A predominantly white school sitting in the middle of a white neighborhood on the southside with predominantly white teachers and staff. None of the Black teachers could I call mine. All my teachers were white. This was Ku Klux Klan infested Jacksonville in the 1980's, which was pretty much southernmost Georgia long before Stacey Abrams "upset" the balance.

Outstanding negro student! Ugh.

As a 17-year-old, I wasn't equipped to deal with something like that. What was I supposed to do with my anger and hurt? Where was I to store it all since I couldn't unleash it all? I was even reluctant to share my hurt with my mum, knowing that the hell she'd raise up at that school with them white folks, ooh chile, would only make things worse for me in the long run. They would have no idea about the wrath of a Black momma over her child, and I never let on to her how badly it hurt.

Besides, the words were already part of the permanent record. Hundreds and hundreds of yearbooks had already been printed. It was a done deal. Even I had advance-ordered and purchased my yearbook. It was supposed to be a memento commemorating my senior year, but white folks had ruined it. Sigh.

I obliterated the caption from my yearbook with a black permanent marker (not then aware of the symbolism) and tried hard to obliterate it from my consciousness as well. The yearbook is in a storage box, heaven knows where. It's been too many years to count since I've set my eyes on it. And I have yet to ever set foot at a high school reunion.

This is me. I only applied to two colleges – Howard University and University of Florida, the former an HBCU, the latter a predominantly white institution. In retrospect, I think that on a deep level I knew something grave was at stake in my choice between Blackness and conditioned whiteness.

I chose Howard University!

One of the best decisions of my life! To be surrounded by Black excellence and beauty, truth, history, celebration, pride, power – just wow! I savored and soaked up every last bit of it.

Thanks to my time at Howard, I was equipped for my foray into the sophisticated "crème de la crème" whiteness of Cornell University, in upstate New York. True to my dual existence and identity, while working toward a doctorate in African-American literature and Shakespeare, I was also mastering "advanced whiteness," a new and different brand than what I had known in the more blatantly racist south. Cornell-level whiteness was the whiteness of "good" white folks who are educated and have cloaked their racism in faux progressivism and moral platitudes. I got to experience how racism cleans itself up and becomes polished, professional, and noticeably more dignified.

This is me. I'm autistic. This is something I say very infrequently to very few people, and this is the first time I've ever written it because I'm still processing this fact after a late-adulthood diagnosis. Several years ago, when my young adult son was formally diagnosed with what is still commonly referred to as Asperger's Syndrome (high-functioning autism), my husband and I began to seriously suspect it about me. It wasn't until I suffered a major panic attack at a major airport that I sought the help of a therapist.

At our very first session, after listening to me and taking notes for over an hour, she repeated back to me my whole life—not the way I had safely said it to her, but the way it was inside of me. Tears were rolling down my face in torrents, and I couldn't speak. She kept looking inside of me, seeing me and reading me, seeing me and reading me. When she was done, she waited for me to speak, but I still couldn't. What she said next would prove to be life-changing.

"Theresa, have you ever been tested for autism? I want to test you for autism."

Oh boy. The tears were back. Tears from a thousand storms rained down my face. It's "raining" now as I write this.

I already knew how the test would come back. My husband knew, too. After my son's diagnosis, we had read up on everything we could get our hands on about autism and had considered me unofficially autistic. Again, only very few people know that I'm autistic because, as I said, I'm still processing it myself and coming to terms with some memories that I had buried.

My mum would frequently scold me over something that I did or something that I said with the words, "You book smart, but you ain't got common sense." Neither she nor I knew that she was commenting on my autistic behaviors and traits. Those words cut deep, and I worked extra hard to learn about common sense and the reason it was bad when it was missing. Again, I was teaching myself to appear neurotypical. I don't recall how long it took me to successfully impersonate a neurotypical person, but it's so habitual now that I still do it.

When you see me or talk to me about this book—and I hope you will, sister—among the two things NOT to say to me are, "You don't look/seem autistic" or "Are you sure?" Please. Just don't.

This is me. I know the hurt and betrayal of a blood sister who, though having shared the same womb and suckled at the same breast, dishonored the will of our father over her lust for money. I no longer believe in the automatic "blood is thicker than water" rule of relationships. I owe her gratitude, however, because she opened my eyes to how one can be a relative but not family. Her betrayal cut me much deeper than any betrayal I've known. I possess no words for it.

In addition to my relatives that I do regard as family, my family also consists of all my Black sisters who embody mutual support, solidarity, and caring, and who like me have ancestors whose family bonds were forcibly severed during their en-slavement as they were forced to watch helplessly as loved ones were ripped from their arms and sold away, powerless to stop it. I cherish our sister bond, and it goes deep.

This is me. I know the betrayal of Black men calling us "bitches" and "hoes," and, who in their desperate longing for patriarchal power and dominance, are among the worst dis- respecters of Black women. Yeah, I said it. At their worst, they are like white women who desire to have everything that white men have—and I do mean EVERYTHING—and will step on, crush, and disavow us to get it. Black men who operate in abusive ways toward Black women possess a misogynist psyche made all the more problematic by chasing whiteness, proximity to whiteness, and "white tail." Yeah, I said it.

This is me. I know the cunning duplicity of white women, who smile in our face when they need support against sexism but are nowhere to be found when they're needed to fight against racism. Nothin.' Nada. Crickets. They expect us to fight alongside them against white men and also side with them against Black men. At the same time, they don't hesitate to weaponize unsuspecting Black men to do their bidding against us when we call out white women on their racist shit.

We see right through white women and their real interests in protecting their white privilege while feigning a superficial interest in fighting for equality. Ha! White women always ditch equality in a hot-white-woman-minute when whiteness is at stake. They want so badly what patriarchy grants white men that they will do anything for proximity to it even if it means getting their pussy[3] grabbed. Sure. They'll suck it up about

---

[3] Black women were more outraged over this misogynist brag than white women who then proceeded to embarrass and shame themselves by voting anyway for the pussy-grabber-in-chief at a rate of 52% in 2016 and an unconfirmed rate of 55% in 2020. The message of white women was clear: "He grabs only the best pussies—ours, the white ones."

being degraded as second-class gender citizens if it means they can be at the top for their whiteness.

It's a no-brainer for me to keep a WWW list – white women to watch list. Yes, I keep an actual list. Trusting them is not automatic, nor does it come easy for me. Their crocodile tears and fake delicateness are deadly to us and to Black men. I prefer to take my chances with white men. It is way too costly to let my guard down with white women.

This is me. This one really pains and disappoints me. I know the betrayal of Black women who have thrown us under the bus because they covet whiteness, proximity to whiteness, and approval of whiteness over Black solidarity and Black sister-hood. Having bought into the white lie that there can be only "one of us," they do the dirty work of their masters and become willing and gullible operatives in our oppression. These are the Black women who make a public showing out of trashing other sisters so that they can receive an approving nod and pat on the head from whiteness.

This is me. I know the rejection of mixed British Jamaican in-laws who prize and identify with whiteness, literally and figuratively. In-laws who, though I'm just as smart as my hus-band (in some areas, smarter) and also Ivy League educated like him, wanted more class for their golden boy than my southern Black U.S. pedigree. It took many years after the birth of our daughter to feel no longer blamed for somehow ruining his life by tripping him up so that he'd "accidently fall penis first into my lady parts." (Thank you, *Big Bang Theory,* for the inspiration for this brilliantly ridiculous line.)

This is me. I know what it's like to have family members jailed under a justice system and mass incarceration system that chews up and spits out Black men for breakfast. And though we know full well about the shady school to prison pipeline, and though we know the Black population has the highest imprisonment rate, jailed family members are often not talked about freely outside of our own families.

This is me. What others meant for evil, God used for my training. My lemons got turned into lemonade, and they also got turned into down-home lemon poundcake, lemon drop cookies, and lemon meringue pie! Guuurrrlll, won't He do it though! And all the time right on time!

I got fired from a lemon job and escorted out of the building because I spoke out against the racism directed at me and sought legal action. My ensuing lawsuit against the company, which I won, fueled my passion for equity and justice and taught me that money, as a language, talks and walks and is power's language of choice. Appeals to morality don't work with die-hard committed white supremacy.

I got fired from another lemon job because I was horrible at hocking company books from the back of the room after training engagements for which I received rave reviews. That experience reaffirmed my commitment to people over profit. It was also a lesson on how soulless and empty a company is when profit is their king. Profit is fleeting; relationships are transforming and transformative.

I left a lemon job because I defied a token Black man in the big house who had sold his soul to white folks. Due to him proving his loyalty to whiteness, I became collateral damage in a "clean house" sweep of an entire department that got demolished by enraged whiteness.

I almost got fired from another lemon job because I refused to suck it up and stay silent about an "everybody knows it," "leadership sanctioned" hot mess white-identifying woman. She brought the company too much profit for them to get rid of her. They let her wreak havoc with no regard for the hell I was going through with her as my manager.

I've gone through a lot of lemon jobs. Some appear on my resume. Some do not. As we know, what white folks view as job-hopping on our resume is oftentimes our choice to leave a hostile work environment— racially hostile or otherwise. If they really wanted to hear the truth about why we REALLY left that job and manager, they wouldn't be all the time telling us to never bad-mouth past employers or to not burn any bridges. All of that is code for keeping us knowing our place, keeping us quiet, and keeping a system that perpetuates us being indebted to and beholden to them for employment. It also gives companies a pass to hold on to nightmare employees and to not make any changes to fix the nightmare environment. In the corporate workplace, there's no such thing as safety with duty to warn—unless anonymously on Glassdoor.

We arrive to our next job interview and instead of being honest about the pure-d hell that our white witch or warlock manager put us through, we come up with the spin that whiteness wants to hear. The spin that reassures them we'll be the pliable negroes that won't make trouble—the negro who they can feel good about hiring. The spin that makes them feel good about saying "culture add" out loud while on the inside they still expect and demand "culture fit." Ugh.

I hated my life in corporate. I hated my life in education. The rule of whiteness is everywhere. For every single job I have ever held, Karens and other white dumbfuckery played a role in my leaving or my firing. Every. Single. One.

This is me. With my not having visited a hair salon since February for my usual hair straightening treatment, I've embarked on a new relationship with my natural hair. As a girl, I had my hair processed with a straightening comb heated on the gas stove top. From there I graduated to a chemical straightener. Does anybody remember the Vigorol one? Whew chile, those chemicals smelled a whole lot worse back then.

Over the years, I've done every kind of thing to my hair except let it be natural! Our new covid reality exposed curly roots I've always had, and I've embraced them. As a mature woman of 50+, I'm learning for the first time how to style my natural hair. I'm also rockin' head wraps and channeling India Arie's "I Am Not My Hair." Pray for me, y'all. A sistah tryna stay with it and keep that relaxer monkey off my back.

This is me. My feelings about the political landscape and regular assaults on democracy in real time while hundreds of thousands die from coronavirus have accelerated the amount of cussin' I'm doing. Exponentially. I can't make it through 5 minutes of the news without yelling "what the fuck?!" about the latest episode in this shitshow we're living. I can't make it through a Houston covid update without wondering out loud "what the actual fuuuccck is wrong with Texas?!" I can't bear to tune in to what's happening in my home state of Florida without screaming, "What the fuck is a DeSantis, and can't they contain it?!" I can't bear to hear the voice of the current big house occupant without calling him "an evil fucking moron!" and screaming at him to "shut the fuck up!" I'm not proud of this. I'm not okay. However, the cussing is better and cheaper than placing big online orders to wine.com. So there's that.

Only through my husband's intervention did I realize that, indeed, I'm dropping F-bombs all over the place as an expression of my volatile emotional state and escalating anxiety levels. I'm even dropping F-bombs unnecessarily. When I can't remember where I put my cell phone, it becomes, "What the fuck did I do with my phone!?" I know. It's bad. People who know me would be shocked. This wasn't me this time last year. Sure, I'd do the basic 3 – the occasional hell, damn, and shit— but not the F-bombs. Again, I'm not okay. If there's a patch for this, I need to get one to help me break the habit. I'm thinking that January 20 could be the day I fuckin' quit cold-turkey.

This is me. Whew! All of this. All. Of. This. My 50+ years have brought me to this moment, and I'm speaking. Silence worked for me until it didn't. So, I'm speaking on race and racism as shapers of my journey—my experiences, my perspective, my thoughts—and which account for my Blaxhaustion.

Blaxhaustion \blaks-ˈzȯs-chən \ Is a Real Thing

Blaxhaustion is my now.

My cumulative now.

I'm popping Aleves like tic-tacs. My facial seborrheic dermatitis has flared up. I've lost weight. My anxiety[4] levels have skyrocketed. I've ordered CBD drops. I'm taking melatonin to try and sleep. Searing hot flashes and incessant night sweats are kicking my ass. I tire more readily. I grow fatigued more easily. My frustration is palpable. My patience is at an all time low. My anger bubbles just below the surface. I'm a ticking time bomb.

And that was all just yesterday.

Now let me tell you about today...

Some days when I'm maxed out on white dumbfuckery, I need a complete "white-out" day.

No matter though what feelings or thoughts dominate my spirit, one thing I feel every day is human. I feel human. And that I even need to affirm humanness and write it here is exhausting. Human. Just human.

Black skin don't make us subhuman or superhuman. So why are we subject to the schism narrative of both? Black skin don't make us weaker or stronger. Black skin don't make us gentler or tougher. We've just had to prove more shit than others have

---

[4] Bonus tip: Telling someone with anxiety disorder to relax and calm down is like telling someone with clinical depression to smile and cheer up. In other words, it's inappropriate and offensive.

had to prove. We've just had to endure more shit than others have had to endure. Plus, the weight of Black girl tax ain't no joke—working twice as hard to be considered half as good and getting shit on constantly.

And don't get me wrong. I get that we have to endure. We have to press onward. We have to stand firm. We have to persevere. We always have to have to! Ugh.

But you know what exists between superhuman (which we're not) and subhuman (which we're not)? Human!

H-U-M-A-N.

I just want to be human and experience and feel all the "normal" non-racism related complexities that come with humanness – the dejection, the uplift, the weariness, the exhilaration, the disappointment, the joy, the sadness, the hope. And I want it all without blaxhaustion.

Blaxhaustion is a deep chronic fatigue unique to us and is the cumulative sum of

ALL the decentering, racial, stereotypical projections of who we are and should be,

ALL the weight of endless racial profiling, racial microaggressions, and racial transgressions,

ALL the blows to our spirit borne of a racist obsession to crush it,

ALL the despair from a lack of compassion and dismissal of our struggles,

ALL the weariness of proving our humanity over and over again,

ALL the simmering restraint to not return evil for evil,

ALL the energy and effort required to take the "professional" or Biblical high road,

ALL the unresolved racial trauma we carry in our DNA.

Blaxhaustion permeates all aspects of our life and is exacerbated by the minimizing or denial of our experiences.

And this year with lockdowns, shutdowns, work-from-home, remote work, Zooming, virtual reality, digital pivot, our blaxhaustion has taken us to the deep guarded places inside ourselves so deep that our bounce-back ain't bouncin' back, our come-back ain't comin' back, our put-up-or-shut-up done packed up.

All of this is NOT a vacation,

NOT a sabbatical,

NOT a retreat,

NOT a honeymoon,

NOT a camping trip,

NOT a staycation.

With our lives, well-being, and "relative safety" disrupted and threatened, we are struggling mentally, emotionally, financially, spiritually, physically, socially.

We are not okay.

None of this is okay.

And, sister, you know how it goes. If we, as Black women, were to take on every single affront and every single offensive comment, we'd be too exhausted for anything else.

I was almost too exhausted to deal with the latest attack, but I decided to just include it here in the introduction. It's truly full circle to have written about the event that sparked this book and then return two months before the launch to relay the "blacklash" that accompanied the announcement of the book's title. Déjà vu. Here we go again. Same shit. different day.

But first, I did not title this book "Let's all sing happy-go-lucky songs and hold hands and be more positive about Black bodies being killed, more positive about systemic racism, more positive about daily affronts to our humanity."

No.

And second, I did not select a cover illustration with rainbows, lucky charms, and smiley faces. My cover depicts a Black woman, the most at-risk among us of being over-shadowed, the most at-risk for threats to safety and well-being.

I have a total of zero fucks to give about white folks' discomfort or offense when I speak or write on topics that center me and Black women.

And I have less than zero fucks to give about white folks getting riled up over my title. And boy, oh boy, did they get riled up and triggered. They were crawling out from under their "professional" rocks and then using the rocks to take aim at MY use of "Karens" in MY title for MY book in MY announcement. See how whiteness works!

The title of my latest book is *Blaxhaustion, Karens & Other Threats to Black Lives and Well-Being. A Black Woman's Perspective.* In it, I wrote what I wrote. Dropping soon. Stay tuned.

There was also a tweet by Kiana King @_trillerina that I used to accompany the announcement.

31

>>> <<<

White women have been calling Black women "Shenaenae," "La'Quisha," and "ShaNiqua in a demeaning manner since the '80's. Latinas were called "Consuela," "Guadalupe," or "Maria." Asian women were called "Ling-Ling," but they can't handle being called Karen for 11 months.

The superiority of whiteness couldn't even see how ironic it was that they were exhibiting classic Karen behavior. I can only imagine the number of social media managers that Karens were calling on to do something about me and my announcement.

And still, I wrote what I wrote.

That was my ready response. My refusal to be baited made things more bearable for me. My detractors had no idea how to respond to that and grew even more infuriated. I envisioned their color changing to red real quick when they read that line!

And oh. I would pay Samuel Jackson good money to record this line for me, "And still, muthafuckas, She. Wrote. What. She. Wrote."

Priceless.

It would be worth every penny. If anybody has a cousin whose best friend's aunt's hairdresser shops at the same grocery store where Samuel Jackson's driver's brother does his grocery shopping, then please hook a sistah up!

Granted, the title contains other words and phrases, but clearly the pro-Karen crowd cares nothing for Black lives and well-being. It's also not concerned about blaxhaustion and other threats we face.

When the mob-like reaction of whiteness activates against us, all bets are off. Whiteness doesn't even pretend to be underground when it feels threatened. Who among us hasn't experienced the mob-like negative reaction of white folks to a perceived or actual threat to whiteness? And whiteness isn't triggered just by perceived or actual slights from Black folks. Whiteness is also threatened by our advances and our excellence. The intent of their targeted "blacklash" is to put us back in our place and restore the racial order.

Not today. I'm not having it. The existing racial order is at the very root of what threatens us, and more than 60 of us are speaking about it.

How This Book Is Organized

Whatever was on my mind and in my spirit to write, that's what I wrote. Some days my anxiety levels were either a help or a hindrance to the process. Though I've reigned in my stream of consciousness via 5 major acts, the scenes themselves may not be as clear-cut. Some scenes are mere snapshots because the sentiment that each conveys is intended to land with a boom without added exposition. Other short scenes embody the energy of lemme-just-say-it-short-and-sweet-cuz-I-can't-even. Some scenes are a bit longer because I had more to say. There's no rhyme or reason to the length of the scenes or their sequence in the acts. From a "literary" perspective, the nature of the scenes is a mirror into my emotional and mental state.

In addition to the five acts with their varying scenes, weaved throughout are poems and the "I'm Speaking" voices of 62 women of the Black diaspora.

Act I focuses on **Blaxhaustion™**, the cumulative exhaustion from a lifetime of racism that impacts our personal and professional life and that manifests emotionally and mentally.

Act II focuses on **Karens, Her Ken, and Her Kin** to shine a light on instances of weaponized whiteness that present a more immediate and impending threat. This act also draws attention to the inconvenient reality of tompromised™ folks who cooperate with whiteness in ways detrimental to Blackness.

Act III focuses on **Coronaviracism™: A Tale of Two Pandemics**, the intersection of covid19 and anti-Black racism, the two pandemics currently ravishing this country.

Act IV focuses on **Great White Lies** that perpetuate and sustain racism and white supremacy.

Act V focuses on **White Complicity & Performative Wokeness**, which emphasizes so-called good white folks and fake allies who put on a show of support with empty words and small gestures—signifying and sacrificing nothing—all while maintaining the benefits of white privilege.

I'm Speaking

Each of us knows what it's like to regularly "have to" navigate and occupy spaces that are low on or VOID of psychological and emotional safety for us. We operate in UNSAFE spaces all the time. And though I dismissed Karen and Candace 'nem with my warning, we all know that some white folks will specifically pick up this book to listen in with no desire to honor our experiences but rather to gaslight us, attack us, and discount our experiences. To them I say, "Be gone. You are not welcome here."

For our accomplices, supporters, and sincere seekers, I urge you to enter these pages with a heart intent on decentering itself, with skin thick enough to need no defenses and thick enough to withstand truth, and with a mind receptive enough to really listen.

Introduction

I am stronger when I'm in the company of my Black sisters. Together we are stronger. In solidarity we have all joined hands and joined voices to speak our individual and collective truths. These pages are our safe space, our hallowed ground.

I extended a special invitation to these voices so that we could affirm for each other to NOT
wait for
plead for
expect for
space to be held for us or space to be given to us.
We've always had the space.
OUR SPACE.
We each are
grabbing hold of it
embracing all of it
standing tall in it
speaking truth in all of it.

Teddi Williams here, and I'm speaking. The Ancestors have given you permission to speak. So speak IT.

Say it. Anyway, you choose. When you don't, most if not all of us lose!

Bask in your glory, Hell, this is your story!

From beautiful pale caramel hues to midnight blues

Elizabeth, Alice, Janie, Odis, Cathryn, Chantelle breathe in me like thunder....no one can put asunder having our say

It's their breaths that clear the way...to say IT

Elizabeth begat Alice, Alice begat Cathryn, Cathryn begat Chantelle, Chantelle begat...well...here is where I pivot

Alice was the praying one, an Eastern Star whose star far outshined time after time, not because of the eastern, northern, southern, nor western stars, she was the embodiment of all the moons and stars and Sun

Cathryn was the headliner who filled up all of the space around her at just the thought of her

Her charm, her wit, her ability to talk shit, yet ever the lady and not a rouge. She spoke circles around the subliminal sounds of racism holding her own...memories. She made her own music, in fact-she was a melodic cathartic sound. And oh her Crown.... Her ability to capture and command the attention, not to be confused with a demand. No! Not Cathryn. Southern belle, daughter of Alice. Spirited Queen Matriarch, holding her Chalice with a Tongue that could bring one callouses

Chantelle a delicate intricately laced and exquisite pattern of tried and true, with a smooth chocolate hue of midnight blue. Heart of gold, words of a cypher speaking in soothing code. An ode to Cathryn's Queendom, and Alice's freedom Generations of these three speak to me...through me, in me, out to me to you

Speak IT

Speak IT

Speak IT

It is not by chance that you, my dear are here. In this space of sacredness. Supportiveness. Cradling consciousness ever aware that now is your stage to speak. It isn't your breath to hold back any longer. Stifle any longer. Bite your tongue any longer. Run as fast as you can to scream what you want to need to long to speak into a pillow, a towel, a rag. Exhausting. And emotionally costly. And we pivot back to who Chantelle begat. Teddi. Teddi [bear] when you're nice, Grizzly [bear] when you're nasty. "Good day" or "Good night" to enlighten some Karens and dismiss most Beckys when the end of the conversation has come to a close.

Nurse by day, Educator and Collaborator by noon, Mother, Grammy to grandKings....doesn't everyone want the prize. I'm not a man, so I couldn't be an Oscar or a Tony. Grammy to my grandKings--the name alone--when they accomplish all that has been breathed into them--they still have the academy in me, so yes they have me, the Prize.

Teddi sat at the feet of Wess, Janie's young King. Janie begat Wess and Mabel...no fable. First fruits of Black Wallstreet, they were-- narrowly surviving Tulsa's 1921 Race Massacre. Descendants of Black Wallstreet, my words, my thoughts, my strides, my work ethic, my sistaQueenness packed with the heat of mayhem, fire, bullets in the street, then and now as the Ancestors speak.

Speaking to and
Through you
In you
Out of you

Protecting you and

Propelling you
Compelling them
Who listen
Some clutching their pearls
As they hurl one more insult
Others hide in their privilege
As the Ancestors catapult us...

Oooo...you hear that?

Hush! (The Ancestors tell them)
Hush! (The Ancestors hail them)
That's my baby....

And she's speaking!

You are them. They are you.

No need to fear, you're in a safe space to close the
case on their dismissive, deflective, flailing, failing
attempts to keep you mute

Borrowed breaths of Ancestor Queens implore you
and fill your lungs shushing others who silenced
them so you can have this platform

Silent no more

Oooo...you hear that?

Hush! (The Ancestors tell them)
Hush! (The Ancestors hail them)

Quiet! (they yell, adjusting their Crowns, a lady
doesn't raise her voice except to protect her child)

That's my baby....

And she's speaking!

Cat, release her tongue. Open your mouth and tell
them with the borrowed, bothered breaths of
10,000's upon 10,000's upon 10,000's Ancestors

Bask in your glory, hell, this is your story!
Now, tell them

I'm speaking

Step up to the plate, sisters...this is your stake

Tell them

You're speaking

You're speaking

You are speaking

The red carpet unfolds for you, inviting you, imploring
you, exploring you, as the Queens you are
Your words are power, not par for the course
Come come come all of you
Each of you

Go 'head, Queen ...and now hold court

What I Hope This Book Will Mean to Black Women

I set out to create a "new thing" with the help of 62 incredible
sistahQueens, and I hope you walk away from this book not
only agreeing, but also feeling that you too are very much a
part of this new thing. Because you are, sister!

Every act,
every scene,
every poem,
every "I'm Speaking" word
prioritizes and centers
US.

This book is our new thing—not fitting into any strict
category or genre. As we speak to and listen to each other,
this book is our stage and audience, our pulpit and congre-
gation, our sermon and choir.

Sistahs, so that we're clear and so that your expectations
are managed, this is NOT a self-help book. It will NOT advise
you on tips and strategies for

- getting a seat at the table
- going high when they go low
- reaching out to willfully ignorant racists

- fitting in with your white colleagues
- kissing the ass of your white boss

That stuff is NOT in the line-up. By design. However, as we engage in this conversation and give voice to our views on threats to our lives and well-being, there may be warnings and general guidance.

As a new thing, this book is many things.

It is a validation and affirmation of our lived experiences, a meeting and relating place, an opportunity to let the world know that we have plenty to say and that they should shut up so we can say it.

It is part of the momentum of #MeToo, an expression and a movement that originated with a Black woman, Tarana Burke, and then was hijacked and "popularized" by white women celebrities like Alyssa Milano and Michelle Williams.

It is part of the momentum of Black Lives Matter, founded by three Black women Patrisse Cullors, Alicia Garza, and Opal Tometi, two of whom identify as queer. At its inception, Black Lives Matter was intended to put LGBTQIA+ voices at the center of the conversation, even while the biggest protests have involved violence against cis hetero Black men.

It is a nod to Black women who've been engaging in activism and speaking for years and years and years, and whose voices are not regarded as "mainstream" or important until whiteness or maleness steps in. It's kinda like the way white feminism has never really served the needs of Black women. Ha! It's exactly the way white feminism has never served the needs of Black women!

It is a symbolic take-off-my-earrings for all the times we've held our tongues in the face of white comfort and white en-titlement.

It is an open letter to a world that has never universally and unequivocally acknowledged that Black lives matter and that Black women's lives matter.

This book just is.

In a practical sense, this book speaks without telling us what we *should* do or how we *should* feel. It doesn't jump in and interrupt to solve problems. It doesn't fix anything. Sound familiar? I hope so. This book is also for all those times that we as Black women want our partners to just listen—really listen—without judgment and without a "fix" but rather listen with support, understanding, and empathy.

This book is a tall cup of tea slowly brewed and scalding hot.

Yaaaasssss!!!!

ACT I

Blaxhaustion

Ya Damn Right We Angry

Actually many of us are looking at angry in the rearview mirror. So let's just get this part out of the way up front before we go any further. Anybody looking for an apology from me for being angry about any of the crap we continue to deal with on a regular basis has a better chance of seeing 45 "be best."

Fact. This country is really fucking racist!

Anger is more than appropriate. Anger at racial inequality, inequity, and injustice is quite appropriate—and necessary.

The more important issue is why aren't more white folks angry?

Hmph. Why don't they turn their attention to addressing the reasons why there hasn't been more outrage from them?

Oh wait...never mind.

Blackness has been and remains criminalized. Our skin color is a crime. Period. Full stop.

Our skin color entitles anyone—including non-Black POC who often side with whiteness against us—to silence us, attack us, kill us.

That we don't regularly act on our anger is good news for our oppressors. Instead, we've spent over 400 years screaming out our worth and value into the universe. That our lives matter is not a debate.

Not partisan.

Not elitist.

Not a contest.

Not a battle cry.

Not exclusionary.

Not a call-and-response.

Black lives matter is an affirmation of our worth and value as a people who were stolen and chained into bondage in this country; legally beaten, raped, tortured, and killed; counted by the Constitution as 3/5 of a person; and denied our basic humanity.

> Dianna Parker here, and I'm speaking. Who died and left white people in charge? Do they have a right to oversee Mother Earth and Her inhabitants? All Anglo-Saxons have done is steal and kill for resources! Yeah, I said it! They create nothing and nurture nothing! If you need to research it...research! Black people have invested too much sweat equity in building this country.

Our very existence is perceived as an affront. Our very lives continue to be devalued, threatened, and taken.

We. Are. Simply. Trying. To. Breathe.

So, yeah, ya damn right we're angry. Justifiably angry. And spirited, and fierce, and intense. If we were to return to white America what it is owed, the picture ain't pretty.

I lost count a long time ago, but I suspect I've saved countless lives by not acting on my anger in ways commensurate with my treatment or the treatment of my loved ones.

We're Not Your Superwoman

> Chris Wright here, and I'm speaking. I am removing my cape; superwoman will no longer be my burden to live up to. Don't hold me to a higher standard; don't tax me extra. SEE ME. HEAR ME. ACKNOWLEDGE ME. I am fearfully and wonderfully made. I am enough as I am.

Let's get a few more things out of the way that have been a long time coming. For centuries now, black women have fought for basic personhood, while white women have been defined as the "fairer sex." We've not been afforded the same privilege to be soft and vulnerable, let alone space to weep or cry. We're not allowed to be angry and tired, frustrated and hopeful, caring and... the entire spectrum of emotions that comprise the human spirit. Multi-dimensional in our emotional depth and capacity, we are nevertheless denied our human-ness.

In the face of trauma and hard times we are expected to throw on our cape and instantly transform into the "Black superwoman." And oh. If we express a contrary view or un-popular view that goes against whiteness, then we morph into—yup, you guessed it—the "angry Black woman."

Our silence they view as threatening.

Our opinion they view as aggressive.

Our disagreement they view as dangerous.

Many of us, regardless of our industry and experience, have been characterized at some point in our career as "difficult to work with." What this usually translates to is that we didn't stay quiet and rollover. We opted instead to speak up against racist bullshit.

Bottomline—we are frequently "othered" into com-partmentalized tropes, stereotypes, and caricatures which further threaten our existence.

> **JeNae Johnson** here, and I'm speaking. I'm my ancestors' wildest dreams and equally, I'm the worst nightmare for any fool who tries to deny the power of the Black woman. I'm trap music meets Bach. I'm corporate strategy meets the Wobble. I'm box braids meets charcuterie boards. I birth Black babies and Black businesses at the same damn time, and my impact is unparalleled. It's undeniable.

Shut Up and Let Me Talk

Mediocre male whiteness can be um...so...well, mediocre. Mediocre doesn't exactly add up to white superiority, so these men have to compensate by taking up all the space. I can still hear Michelle Obama saying this about them, "They're really not that smart." Chile, that became one of my go-to's in our "the look" playbook.

Try it. Say the words to yourself about that jerk and feel yourself *becoming instantly fluent* in how to say it without saying it. I'm channeling that best-seller of hers, *Becoming*. For some reason, the name I always end up choosing for my practice sessions is Bob.

Bob, you're really not that smart.

I like to add a bit of flavor sometimes to mix it up and keep myself entertained. It's my clap-back porn for whiteness.

Bye Bob, witcho mediocre man self.

When I say the words to myself, they really do dictate the facial expression and puts the right accent just where it needs to be!

Anyway, when I'm interrupted, talked over, condescended to, disregarded, or dismissed by a white man who wraps his mediocre-ness in patriarchal entitlement, guuurrrrlllll, I start speaking in tongues with my eyes and energy.

To "dare" to call him out and counter is to be labeled with all the coded and loaded misogynoir words that have been reserved just for us.

I just wanna say to all of them sometimes, "Sit down and shut up."

The sit-down-and-shut-up part, alongside learn how to de-center yourself, is a prerequisite to them speaking up and taking anti-racist action. Their shut-up should definitely not be a permanent state. But it is a necessary first step that they miss—either because they're unwilling or unable. Sometimes as part of my clap-back porn, I envision duct tape. Just sayin' Cuz the more they talk, the more it means bad news for us.

Un-Okayness Is a Thing

Yeah. I don't care how weird it looks on paper or sounds on the tongue. Un-okayness is a thing. When white folks have it, it's legitimized and called chronic fatigue syndrome. But when our ancestors had it, it was called "laziness." And when we have it, we're not even taken seriously.

To be Black is to be un-okay. Whether we explain it or not, or whether we justify it or not, does not change the reality. Whiteness, however, will seek to minimize and dismiss our pain because to do so is easier and more convenient than owning up to the clusterfuck that got us here.

Black women especially have had to smile, be patient, be accommodating, be professional, be nice, and be reasonable about our oppression and never ever appear angry.

It's 2020 and they're still debating whether Black lives matter, they're still mocking Black Lives Matter, and they're still degrading Black Lives Matter.

I am angered, saddened, disgusted.

I remain un-okay.

I regularly experience unexpected bursts of realness, jaw-breaking moments of raw emotions, shocking instances of very strong language, and episodes of justifiable homicidal rage.

I have inadvertently saved many white feelings through my self-isolation.

> **Ashley McGirt** here, and I'm speaking. I am not here to make you comfortable! Breonna Taylor and George Floyd weren't comfortable. Being comfortable looks like Black death! I am here to make you think. I am here to make you unlearn, re-learn, and learn again! I am here to promote the importance of Black wellness, because it hasn't been considered important throughout the history of America.

When Peace is Their Trigger

In 1619, we wanted peace, and they chose slavery. They believed that labelling us weak, inferior, and undeserving meant we deserved to suffer at their hands.

In 1865 we wanted a peaceful end to slavery, and they chose Civil War. They believed that nothing should interfere with their right to prosper at our expense.

During Reconstruction we attempted to peacefully make a life for ourselves and build communities. They chose lynchings, bombings, the Tulsa Massacre, and the Red Summer of 1919, whereby they rioted and murdered us in more than three dozen cities. They felt that we should be taught a lesson for aspiring to thrive in their midst.

During the Civil Rights era when we were trying to peacefully secure our civil rights, they opted to murder our leaders. They have never wanted us to organize and topple the house of cards that whiteness built.

During encounters with the police when we peacefully threw up our hands, they chose to gun us down. They live by the credo that "the only good nigger is a dead nigger."

When we go to church to worship and pray in peace, they execute us. Love and goodwill toward all humankind have never been what they pray for at the arkkk of their covenant with whiteness.

When Kaep exercised his right to peacefully protest, they punished him, called him a villain and a son-of-a-bitch, and locked him out of a career. When Kenosha Kkkyle killed and wounded 3 protestors, they hailed him a patriot and bailed him out of jail on $2M bond.

When Ahmaud Arbery went for an afternoon jog, they hunted and gunned him down like a dog. Like their ancestors of yesteryear, hunting and killing niggers is sport. The only thing missing this time was the commemorative photo and a piece of his flesh cut away as a memento of the occasion.

When Breonna Taylor slumbered peacefully in her bed at night, they barged in and fired bullets into her body. They like to remind us that nothing belongs to us and that we own nothing. Violation, killing, or seizure of Black bodies and Black property is their entitlement.

When Jacob Blake attempted to peacefully leave a situation, they fired 7 bullets into his back at close range while his children watched. They send a message of terror to entire families just like they did for our ancestors who were forced to watch in horror as their loved ones were whipped, beaten, or killed.

When George Floyd peacefully surrendered, the face of whiteness in a blue uniform and badge put a knee to his neck for 8 minutes and 46 seconds and waited for his life to drain out of him. 8 minutes and 46 seconds. Jesus wept. And so did we.

And the list goes on and on and on. Our efforts at peace and peaceful co-existence through the years have been consistently met with violence and brutality.

I can't imagine what they could point to that justifies white as a superior race—unless superior refers to stealing, killing, and destroying.

I do know, however, all that we can point to that justifies our trauma and our overall un-okayness.

> **Themum Crawford** here, and I'm speaking. I am tired! Soooo freaking tired of pretending that everything is gonna be all right. That's what I've always heard, "just be patient." HELL...how much patience can one endure when my brothers and sistahs are constantly hurting, ridiculed, misunderstood, hated, labeled, emasculated...KILLED. I can't BREATHE! Makes me wanna holla...throw up both my hands! Ooo Lawd!

Spare me the White Defensiveness

Some days I am so fatigued from all the bullshit that I have to take a "white out" day. What that means is that I can't bear to watch, listen, or see whiteness showing up in any part of my day.

Though with my words I often don't make a distinction between whiteness and white folks and end up conflating the two, but in terms of my "white out" day, it can very well be Black folks wearing whiteness that I need to avoid. Ugh.

> **Lynne Stokes** here, and I'm speaking. I have every right to be mad. To scream every day if I wanted. Because of all the hell, dismissive behavior, passed overness, and basic invisibility that I have felt over the years. But I choose strength. And intelligence. And beauty. And joy. Too many gave up too much before me to let you win.

AGAIN...It is a blatant devaluing of us and our lived experiences when white folks tell us they are tired of hearing about racism. Do they even consider what it must be like to be tired from a lifetime of experiencing it?!? Their smug indifference is worthy of earring-removal at minimum.

Plus they gaslight the issue by pointing to our use of "white people" and accusing us of divisiveness. They want their white cake and want to eat it too while smashing a piece in our face for good measure. Okay, lemme see if I got this right. They devised the system of Black and white but don't want to be called white.

Okay, Jan.

They benefit from racism but don't want us to call attention to their benefits because they didn't ask for the benefits.

Sure, Jan.

They devised the system of racism but don't want us to call it racism because to do so is divisive.

That's a good one, Jan!

Do they know what's actually divisive?!? FUCKING RACISM, that's what!!

Dating back to the beginning when we were snatched and dragged here, we've been mistreated, maligned, dismissed, censored, attacked, beaten, fired, raped, hanged, choked, kneed, shot—all without the warranted significant sustained changes in racial equity and justice.

As they are the perpetrators, supporters, bystanders, and benefactors of anti-Black racism, They. Don't. Get. To. Tell. Us. That. They're. Tired. Of. Hearing. About. It.

Ever.

We've never lived in a world where we have the luxury of not talking abut race. Our race is one of the most visible things about us. The thing that they initially cooked up to justify enslaving us.

So, yeah. We're beyond tired of experiencing racism, and we have zero fucks to give that they are tired of hearing about it. Literally, racism makes us sick—physically, emotionally, and mentally sick.

The best way for them to shut us up is to dismantle the system and then commit to purging it from hearts and minds.

> **Deloria Nelson Streete** here, and I'm Speaking. I am Love, Power and Beauty. I'm not here to make you comfortable but to speak my truth in love so that you may learn and acknowledge my power, purpose & beauty. It's time to get your knee off of our necks and let us thrive in our beautiful, badass melanated perfection.

We Useta Be Black Girls

The year 2020 has given us much, and it's also given us the death of one of the killers of our Birmingham church girls. Thomas Blanton, Jr., the last living murderer, died June 26. He died unrepentant. He died with his hate. He and his hate died in prison at the age of 84. Until his arrest, he lived free with his hate for 38 years—38 years!—after the 1963 murders until his conviction in 2001. Because...Alabama.

Blanton's hate took the lives of our beloved girls—Addie Mae Collins (age 14), Cynthia Wesley (age 14), Carole Robertson (age 14), and Carol Denise McNair (age 11)—who were attending church that September Sunday morning in Birmingham, Alabama. Church has traditionally been our sacred and safe place to get away from the daily assaults of white supremacy, a place to seek the solace and comfort of our faith.

But no one knew what evil was lurking outside determined to shatter a sanctuary and offer up on the altar of white supremacy the innocent lives of four young girls about the business of changing into their choir robes. I can almost hear them scurrying about possibly giggling innocently the way girls sometimes do, oblivious to the fact that they would soon be sleep in the Lord.

They were four young precious Black girls whose lost lives and value were a fight for justice.

Four Black girls.

Say their names.

Addie Mae Collins.

Cynthia Wesley.

Carole Robertson.

Carol Denise McNair.

Breonna Taylor useta be a Black girl.

Say her name.

We usta be Black girls.

Black girls with dreams and goals that didn't include a hash-tag.

Obtaining justice for our lives seems to result in protracted fights for justice.

It's 2020, and the fight for the worth and value of our lives continues. We're up against the criminalization of our Blackness that starts early. And for Black girls, it involves tactics directed at both behavior and sexuality.

> **Baylie Robinson** here, and I'm speaking. I'm not your sweetheart. I'm not your dear. I'm not your love. Call me by my name and quit instructing me to smile. Beauty is not an equal trade-off in lieu of my intelligence. Black women are much more than a fantasy you've created in your head.

Black girls are viewed as more suspicious, mature, provocative, and aggressive than their white girl classmates. Some of us were lucky enough to have at least one Black teacher during our formative years but others of us may have fallen victim to teachers like one of mine. I was the only Black kid in Ms. Pettijohn's class (yaasss gurl, her real name), and during late spring of my senior year she had me removing gum from the undersides of all the desks. My offense? I was the only one who didn't participate in the traditional senior skip day (that's another story altogether).

As I was the only student to show up to her class that day, I guess she must have been at a loss to figure out what to do with me, so what "brilliance" did she come up with? Punishment! This bitch actually determined that the best thing to do with me was to assign me a humiliating task that she believed was more appropriate than…say, I dunno, maybe engaging me in intellectual conversation about the assigned reading. Ugh! She even had the caucacity to be smiling in her role as "overseer" as she watched me carry out the task. She secured an early spot on my WWW list – white women to watch. Even at age 17, I knew.

When it comes to our girls, it continues to be a battle. Karen-esque teachers have access to the souls and minds of our children for up to six hours a day, five days a week. This often means that our children's teachers spend more time daily with our kids than we do.

For Karens with nefarious purposes, the classroom (virtual or otherwise) is a goldmine. Not only are there more Karen teachers for the younger ones, but the statistics are also very disturbing. "Black girls are over 5 times more likely than white girls to be suspended, 7 times more likely to receive multiple out-of-school suspensions than white girls, and 3 times more likely to receive referrals to law enforcement."[5]

Karen and Ken teachers missed our memo advising "nevah evah mess with the child of a Black mama." It won't end well for them. And yet, they remain a threat to our daughters.

We Useta Be Black Girls (Girlhood Chants)

My mama

Yo' mama

Live across the street

18, 19 Alligator Street

Every night they have a fight

And this is what they say

They say eenymeenydisaleeny

oohlathumbaleena

otchycotchydevarotchy

I love you

Oh baby, yes, I do

Have a peach

---

[5] "A Battle for the Souls of Black Girls," by Green, Erica L, Mark Walker, and Eliza Shapiro. New York Times. 10/01/2020.

Have a plum

Have a stick of chewin' gum

Don't want it

Don't take it

Shake it high

Shake it low

Shake it out the back door

〉〉〉 〈〈〈

Miss Mary Mack Mack Mack

All dressed in black, black, black

With silver buttons, buttons, buttons

All down her back, back, back

She asked her mother, mother, mother

For fifteen cents, cents, cents

To see the elephant, elephant, elephant

Jump the fence, fence, fence

It jumped so high, high, high

That it touched the sky, sky, sky

And it won't come back, back, back,

Til the 4th of Ju-ly ly ly ly ly ly ly ly ly

Damned if You Do (Feel) and Damned if You Don't (Feel)

There is a danger to losing hold of our ability to be surprised and shocked by what's going on around us. The danger is that the horrors and atrocities committed against our humanity become normalized.

We know the stakes are too high to risk being lulled into numbness. Knowing doesn't change how we feel. If anything, the knowing adds an extra layer of blaxhaustion. Being numb can kill us. Getting and staying outraged can kill us.

There is nothing normal about any of this.

> **Vanessa Womack** here, and I'm Speaking. If Fannie Lou Hamer only knew how powerful her words would resonate today, "sick and tired of being sick and tired," to ring so ominously true. Blaxhaustion raises the level of anxiety. Yet there's hope. We must not be silent. We must remain strong, unyielding, and persevere in TRUTH!

WTF?!

Language, which is my art, my activism, my weapon – has now also become my vice. I'm even pulling out my special occasion Jamaican cuss words (one of the perks of being married to a

Jamaican) for the extreme dumbfuckery going on around us –
"what the bumboclaat!" and "the orange rassclaat!"

Rhaatid! Wah a gwaan wid yuh, 2020? Bumbo! Mek yuh
stey so? Yuh rass!

Language Matters

"Do you want to file a complaint?"

"No. I want to right a wrong."

Even the language and how it's used is blaxhausting. The
amount of energy that goes into correcting majority held con-
ceptions makes my teeth hurt.

When I point out an injustice or self-advocate, that is NOT
synonymous with complaining. The overtly negative conno-
tation of "complaining" plays right into the many negative
tropes about Black women being angry or having an attitude
problem. Yes, we do have plenty reasons to be angry, but I
digress...

Seeking justice for an injustice or seeking to right a wrong
is a noble pursuit.

Advocates are not complainers.

Advocates are advocates.

Code Switchers (A Poem)

code-switchers

shape-shifters

duality-bingers

soul-tillers

black-tax victors

Blaxhaustion

long before the 'Rona

we wore the mask

making us agreeable and safe

surviving instead of thriving

the mask can't save us from

voice-nullers

culture-busters

history-scrubbers

hate-pushers

truth-snuffers

yet we wear the mask

so we can breathe

and teach our kids the same

—\o/ tmr

Read My Face

Our very own language. The Black woman's facial expression also known as "the look." We use it with our family and friends, with Black men, and with white folks who try our last nerve.

That last category is the one that .... Whew chile, I can't even finish that thought.

The loud look language is for those times when my voice and humanity have been threatened and denied, when I'm feeling like I have to tip-toe to avoid the "angry Black woman" trope, when I'm really struggling to maintain my composure, and when I'm holding back the emotion and clap-back that the moment calls for.

> **Tanesha Kelly** here, and I'm speaking. A professional, educated, black woman who will no longer allow small-minded individuals of today's society to overlook my worth simply because YOU cannot admit that my skin color will never define my intelligence and strong work ethic. I am significant in every way. My power is in my voice.

And still, after pushing through and persevering through ALL THAT and jumping through the man-made hoops, the leader of the free world can come along and in a single two-line tweet reduce Kamala Harris to "monster" by the "supreme power of man-ness."

The "monster" narrative plays into the white wheelhouse of not human at worst and 3/5 human at best. The cruel irony of past and present is that whiteness is the monster. White folks, in the name of whiteness, have committed and perpetuated upon us the most unspeakable horrors and atrocities.

I Can't Even

The "all lives matter," and "blue lives matter" rebuttals are a distraction and a deflection. Blue lives aren't even a thing. Except in the world of *Avatar*. So yeah, fiction. Made up racist crap to justify modern-day slave patrols' "right" to kill Black folks. So let's just dispense with this brand of "blue is the new white" stupid right here.

Okay, so back to this "all lives matter" retort that white folks love so much. They know it's triggering for us, and we'll likely take the bait. The energy we devote to explaining over and over again steals focus away from real equity and justice work by manufacturing a shiny new thing for us to chase and fight. I know cuz I was constantly allowing myself to get baited. Engaging with this foolishness keeps us explaining the minimum— that our lives matter—repeatedly.

For more than too long they've said we had little to no value. And we've spent more than too long proving that we do. I don't know about you, but I'm so done with this. If white folks can't clear this low bar in their thinking, I'm not the one. I gladly give them over to any of my sisters and brothers who are more equipped with this brand of willful ignorance and committed stupid. If they can't be convinced that there are things more important than being white, why in the world would they concede that our lives matters. And let's not even talk about that whole "white lives matter" foolishness. That alone is an entire book!

They know full well that our lives matter. But they refuse to do better when they know better. Consider the countless historical and present-day receipts of bodily theft, intellectual property theft, and cultural appropriation.

They know.

They've always known. A self-proclaimed "superior" race would not feign ignorance unless it serves their agenda in upholding the status quo. Think about it. Guuurrrlll, they rage against our greatness because our greatness exposes the great lie of whiteness.

And so, I'm no expert or anything but all these instances of "superior" white folks having meltdown episodes of rage in public spaces and on social media don't seem to quite square up with that white supremacy nonsense they keep serving up. Hmph.

Linkkkedln and Social Media Oppression[6]

The main distinction between the professional networking social media platform and all the others is that with LinkedIn, racism shows up with a briefcase, suit and tie or heels. But oh, the irony of a well-dressed racism that so blatantly exposes itself. A dressed-up pig is still a pig, and we don't have long to wait for it to return to wallowing in and slinging mud.

Make no mistake. LinkedIn is a "sundown" platform, much like the sundown cities where Black folks who show their faces after dark fall victim to the evil of white folks. In other words, when entering this white platform, we had better respect boundaries and not show up Black. Violations are met with suppression, silencing, and banishment by law-and-order algorithm patrols and also by law-and-order human patrols when things escalate. And by escalate, I mean when we get "uppity" and ask questions.

---

[6] The same folks who say to us, "Well if you hate this country so much, then leave" are the same folks that will say, "If LinkedIn is so bad, then leave." My response to these folks is simple—I have a right to be here. Neither citizenship nor membership exempts entities from the criticism of their citizens or members.

> **Lisa Hurley** here, and I'm speaking. The algorithms are busy. The people who create, code, and manage the algorithms—and their respective platforms—are busy. Busy silencing Black voices. Busy amplifying racist voices. Busy suppressing the truth. Busy promoting propaganda. Despite this, I believe that, ultimately, we anti-racists will prevail. So we, too, must stay busy. That's why no matter how tired I get, I continue to #DoTheWork.

With all the troping and stereotyping of Black women, I guess not enough folks have read the anecdotal memo. We clap back. More and more of our voices are rising up with greater determination. When one of us is shut down, at least five more of us will rise up.

It's not something I'm exactly proud of, but I'm also fluent in nice-nasty and snark. And I use both if all else reasonable fails.

I am so over it when it comes to male trolls who have nothing better to do than show off their inadequacies and insecurities by attacking us on social media with that rare blend of racism and misogyny—misogynoir.

Trumpism and a MAGA-cult mentality have given mediocre white men especially the bold license to spew their nonsense with impunity.

Why?

It's simple.

Three words.

Because. They. Can.

Hate is trending.

So I do what we do when we do what we do—take matters promptly into our own hands and ignore, delete, block, report, clap back, name, shame. When they go low, our voices grow.

> **LeNeice Gavin** here, and I'm speaking. I find it quite offensive when white men and women state that I am "different" from other Black people. You know, like I should somehow feel flattered that they perceive me as being "greater than" the "less than" perception they obviously hold towards us as a whole. That, and the white women who recently attempted to pass for black. WTF!

Assembly Not Required

Back in the day, when they thought too many of us were occupying a space, we were considered threatening at worst and worrisome at best. One of the best books on racism by psychologist and educator Beverly Tatum even emphasized whites' concern about self-segregation in its title, *Why Are All the Black Kids Sitting Together in the Cafeteria?*

Today, it takes only one of us to instill in them an irrational hate and fear. What that translates to is that any one of us can be the victim of whiteness any time, any place, *for any reason*.

Law, legal tenet, and procedure bolster that last part.

Stand-Your-Ground Law.

Think George Zimmerman who shot and killed 17-year-old Trayvon Martin.

Citizens Arrest.

Think Gregory and Travis McMichael, the father and son duo, who shot and killed Ahmaud Arbery.

Self-defense and proper procedure claims of pattyrollers knockin' down the door of a private home in the middle of the night.

Think Jonathan Mattingly, Brett Hankison, and Myles Cosgrove, the home-raiding cops, who shot and killed Breonna Taylor.

In addition to all that, they've also perfected the justification used by law enforcement, vigilantes, neighborhood patrols, Karens, etc.

"I feared for my life."

It has become the "get out of accountability free card."

All the shooters were fearful of their lives.

All the shooters were the aggressors.

All the shooters were the initiators.

All the victims were unarmed.

All the victims were engaged in innocuous non-threatening activities.

One was walking home from the store.

One was jogging through the neighborhood.

One was sleeping in her home.

Let's do the math.

White fear plus white-determined laws and white-controlled everything equal murdered Black bodies.

> **Tiana Conley** here, and I'm speaking. Isn't it ironic that a world/ society/ workplace that actively conspires against Black women, also enlists us to provide solutions to our oppression that are deemed acceptable by systems of white supremacy? Don't fall for it sistahs. We must fight for freedom, justice, and equality according to our own truths, our own experiences, and on our own terms!

Our House but Their Rule

The most disrespected person in America is the black woman. The most unprotected person in America is the black woman. The most neglected person in America is the black woman.

—Malcolm X

There's no place like home. Unless the home is ours. Home was sorta kinda the last frontier of safety for us, the place where we could let our hair down literally and figuratively and keep the threat of whiteness at bay.

My favorite room in my house I consider my sanctuary. My preferred space of relaxation, calm, and rest. And most of all, safety and security.

So, serious question, sisters. Are there any "safe spaces" in existence for us on this earth in this lifetime? I'm fine with this place not being my forever home, but can I please, Lawd, not get shot before I make it outta here? And please can my family members and friends not get shot?

Blaxhaustion

Breonna Taylor is not the first one of us to have the sanctity of her home breached and violated by whiteness. Not the first of us killed while homing. I want her to be the last.

Say her name.

Kathryn Johnson, killed by police at home, 2006

Aura Rosser, killed by police at home, 2014

Michelle Cusseaux , killed by police at home, 2015

Janisha Fonville, killed by police at home, 2015

Atatiana Jefferson, killed by police at home, 2019

Breonna Taylor, killed by police at home, 2020

> **Thordis Howard** here, and I'm speaking. The weight of my skin feels like a suit of armor, yet it provides me no protection. No camouflage from predators. In fact, my brown complexion is the cause of my oppression. I bear this load without reprieve along my quest toward the American dream. Burdened by the skin I'm in.

That "Stand By" Whistle

Not even coded this time. Smdh. An explicit call-out to hate-mongering white men with toxic energy for them to keep their finger on the trigger. White men who brandish their hate with guns that, by the way, are more a symbol for their insecurity and irrational fear than they are a sign of power and strength.

Stand by.

Two carefully chosen words to call up the fear and the trauma that we carry from our ancestors who endured the most atrocious horrors inflicted on them by Bible-thumping Christian slavers.

What non-targeted safe folks heard as "stand by," the rest of us heard as "kill Black folks when I give you the go-ahead."

As the saying goes, "That ain't nothin' but the devil."

Terrifying.

Virtual Life and Death

I attended my first Zoom funeral with my husband. The dearly departed was the father of his cousin's husband. Neither of us knew him personally but wanted to show our support. More than 250 attended – or rather, more than 250 screens were in attendance because some screens showed entire families who had solemnly gathered in front of their computer cameras to pay tribute and respect. My husband and I were a "plus one" for our screen.

As I sat watching and listening to each tribute, something strange happened. Tears started falling from my eyes, first a trickle or two, and then they were streaming down my face. And like water leaking from a broken faucet, I couldn't turn it off. The tributes had triggered my brokenness, my frustration, and my desire to scream wtf and bumboclaat at the top of my lungs. Brokenness mixed with anger.

The next day was Monday. After waking, getting dressed, doing my hair and make-up, s l o w l y I ascended the stairs to enter our in-home studio to deliver a virtual workshop to a group of engineers that included no Black folks and very few POC.

Thank God it wasn't a new group, but rather a returning leadership team for their third workshop in a series. Even still though, among the first words I delivered to them as part of my standard greeting and introduction spoke volumes.

"I am not okay. The Black community is not okay. Though I, as your facilitator, will continue to prioritize your safety, I will NOT prioritize your comfort."

If it were an in-person session, I might be tempted to describe what happened next as "not hearing a pin drop." In this case, guuurrrrlllll, I think everybody's screen froze!! Never do I recall a group—especially a group of mostly white male leaders!—so quick to agree with every concept or insight I shared with them thereafter. Sister, I am chuckling to myself now thinking about it. Not a single person posed a contrasting view. I guess they were picking up on my "don't fuck with me today, white people" energy. Of course, *they* wouldn't call it that, but even in a Zoom environment, they knew.

Two hours doesn't seem like a long time, but when I'm the one who is feeling split between confident and uneasy in a space where no one looks like me and I'm the lead, the adrenaline and stress hormones just wear me down. When the adrenaline wears off, I usually crash down heavy and have to retreat to my bed with two Aleves.

Say Their Names (A Tribute)

Know our terror. Know our trauma. Know that our dead-and-gone greatly outnumber these 54 souls. These are just the

73

ones we know about. Seeing and saying their names have a greater impact than a statistic citing the numbers alone. These murdered souls are mothers and fathers, daughters and sons, sisters and brothers. Their lives had meaning. Each had hopes and dreams. Each life held the promise of possibilities to now never be fulfilled.

By the time you hold this book in your hands, odds are there will be more souls to add to this list. I don't want to be right, but am I? Are you reading this with the knowledge that there's been "another one"? Cuz you know that's how we refer to our struck-down sisters and brothers. "Another one." Smdh.

Angelo "AJ" Crooms
Sincere Pierce
Marcellis Stinnette
Jonathan Dwayne Price
Dijon Durand Kizzee
Rayshard Brooks
Carlos Carson
David McAtee
Tony "Tony the Tiger" McDade
George Perry Floyd
Michael Brent Charles Ramos
Daniel T. Prude
Breonna Taylor
Manuel "Mannie" Elijah Ellis
William Howard Green
Ahmaud Arbery
Sean Reed
Botham Jean
Atatiana Jefferson
Jonathan Ferrell
Renisha McBride

Blaxhaustion

Stephon Clark
Jordan Edwards
Jordan Davis
Alton Sterling
Aiyana Jones
Mike Brown
Tamir Rice
Reverend Clementa Pinckney
Cynthia Hurd
Reverend Sharonda Coleman-Singleton
Tywanza Sanders
Ethel Lance
Susie Jackson
Depayne Middleton Doctor
Reverend Daniel Simmons
Myra Thompson
Trayvon Martin
Sean Bell
Oscar Grant
Sandra Bland
Philando Castile
Corey Jones
John Crawford
Terrence Crutcher
Keith Scott
Clifford Glover
Claude Reese
Randy Evans
Yvonne Smallwood
Amadou Diallo
Walter Scott
Eric Garner
Freddie Gray

My Black Mother's Lens

My lens is not like the lens of white mothers and fathers. White women view my twenty-something-year-old son as a threat. The same threat that an 18-year-old Black youth was thought to be as he rode his bike to basketball practice—a bike that a self-identified "white Hispanic" assumed he stole.[7] Remember that?

The white Hispanic, operating as a vigilante, stopped the 18-year-old, who was "appropriately" apologetic and kept his hands up and visible the whole time—behaviors very familiar to me as a Black mother.

I teach these behaviors. To my son. He has been instructed on and "certified" in "How to Stay Alive 101." I hate that this is the reality of parenting a Black child, but as we all know, we don't have the luxury of not addressing the horrors of being targeted for the color of our skin.

As for their education? You know.

It includes the compliant demeanor.

It includes the tone of deference, with some variable "yes sirs" thrown in if needed.

It includes the safe way to show-your-hands stance.

It includes the say-and-do-whatever-it-takes-to-stay-alive strategies.

Does teaching our son this stuff disgust and anger me to no end? Do I hate drilling this pre-trauma into him?

Yes, definitely!

The alternative scenario that we've witnessed over and over again convinces us that the immediate priority is for him

---

[7] "Florida Man Accused of Illegally Detaining Black 18-Year-Old Heading to Basketball Practice." Christina Carrega. abcnews.com. 07/29/2020.

to stay alive in the moment and then join us in the fight for justice in the next moment.

> **Jo Bonsell** here, and I'm Speaking. Listen, if you desecrated my land, degraded my femininity, and attempted to destroy my history and be the cause of death to my son and I ain't laid down and died yet, I'd be scared as hell of me, too. Besides, I am your MOTHER!

Because my son is autistic, it makes him especially vulnerable to being accused of disrespect (his bluntly honest speech) and suspiciousness (his avoidance of eye contact), both of which can prompt a trigger-happy pattyroller to fear for his life and gun down my son. And so we take that into consideration when we do the drills and have the talks.

My sister worries that her son will forget the lessons in the moment due to his indignation at the injustice of being stopped while Black. No mother should have to worry about this. None of us should have to worry about this.

That we all want our children to stay alive in that moment is what unites us. My hope is that one day there will be a just world where our children can be children and not worry about the skin they're in being regarded as a weapon.

Until that day comes, a traumatized child is better than a dead one. It's better to console my terrified child than to bury him.

According to Stephanie Coradin, a sistahQueen from Haiti, Haitians have a saying that translates to "it's better for a child to cry than for a parent to HAVE TO cry." Ain't that the truth.

The 18-year-old who was simply riding his bike to basketball practice survived the encounter, thank God. And still, I weep in anguish a mother's tears for him. I am utterly and completely undone thinking about our children in the world we inhabit and our inability to protect them 24/7.

I Cannot Sell You This Painting (A Poem)[8]

I cannot sell you this painting. In her expression, I see the Black mothers who are unseen, and rendered helpless in this fury against their babies.

As I listlessly wade through another cycle of violence against Black people,
I paint a Black mother...
eyes closed,
furrowed brow,
holding the contour of her loss.
Is this what it means for us?
Are black and loss
analogous colors in America?
If Malcolm could not fix it,
if Martin could not fix it,
if Michael,
Sandra,
Trayvon,
Tamir,
Breonna and
Now George Floyd...
can be murdered
and nothing changes...

---

[8] Artist Titus Kaphar painted a portrait—of a Black mother holding the outline of her baby—that appeared on the June 15 cover of Time Magazine. This poem accompanied it.

wouldn't it be foolish to remain hopeful?
Must I accept that this is what it means to be Black
in America?
Do
not
ask
me
to be
hopeful.
I have given up trying to describe the feeling of knowing
that I can not be safe in the country of my birth...
How do I explain to my children that the very system set
up to protect others could be a threat to our existence?
How do I shield them from the psychological impact of
knowing that for the rest of our lives we will likely be seen as
a threat,
and for that
We may die?
A MacArthur won't protect you.
A Yale degree won't protect you.
Your well-spoken plea will not change hundreds of years
of institutionalized hate.
You will never be as eloquent as Baldwin,
you will never be as kind as King...
So,
isn't it only reasonable to believe that there will be no
change
soon?
And so those without hope...
Burn.
This Black mother understands the fire.
Black mothers
understand despair.

I can change NOTHING in this world,
but in paint,
I can realize her....
This brings me solace...
not hope,
but solace.
She walks me through the flames of rage.
My Black mother rescues me yet again.
I want to be sure that she is seen.
I want to be certain that her story is told.
And so,
this time
America must hear her voice.
This time
America must believe her.
One
Black
mother's
loss
WILL
be
memorialized.
This time
I will not let her go.

—Titus Kaphar

ACT II

Karens, Her Ken, and Her Kin

Open Letter to White Women

Not all white women are active Karens, so I want to address a certain group of white women who've consistently voted against any ticket that is aligned with working toward equity and equality—at rates as high as 55%! (For the record, white women absolutely suck at voting against whiteness.) As we know, along with Karen, these white women are no more aligned with us and our cause than are white men. And in fact, in many circumstances, white feminists have shown themselves to be more of a danger and threat.

Even if there were a guarantee that not a single white woman would pick up this book, I'd still include this letter. The writing of it felt like a much-needed therapeutic exercise. Like a letter I'd write to someone who has passed on, this letter is for release, for closure, and for the articulation of things not said. In short, this letter combines my utterance with the utterance of hundreds of years. The utterance of yesterday and today. The utterance of countless sisters and sistahQueen ancestors.

Dear white women,

We've grown so very tired of waiting for you to get your shit together. You've been playing your little innocent act for far too long. You ain't fooling nobody but yourself and the gullible men of all races that can't see right through you. Your cunning and savvy surpass mediocre man-ness, but not so for us though. We see you. Black women have always had your number.

You've been wreaking havoc in our lives since the time of our enslaved ancestors. You showed us who you were that first time when you heaped terrible abuse on us when you thought no one else was looking, when, instead of recognizing, empathizing with, and defending our oppressed and power-less plight, you punished us when your white men repeatedly raped us. Their crime was your shame too, and you beat us for it.

We also know your dirty little secret. The one that nobody talks about. The one that the history books forgot to mention when they footnote the fact that your white men impregnated our ancestors. What about you though? To hide your carnal desire for enslaved Black men, you enticed them to lay in your whiteness to satisfy your forbidden lust. Denying you was not their option if they wanted to live. Their refusal would be met with your torn garments and cries of rape. You are the con-summate liar. You knew full well they'd be tortured and killed by white men enraged at even the slightest suggestion of your sullied and violated pristine feminine whiteness.

What did you do with the babies you birthed whose melanated skin was the evidence of your sin? Did you even for a split-second think about how you could pass the baby off as the progeny of your white husband in order to save the life of your baby? What did you tell him when after nine months of watching you swell with what he believed was his seed resulted in a "stillborn"? Did he even ask to see the baby and say good-bye? And oh, what smart and cunning response did you have ready for him? Did you demand our ancestors keep their mouths shut or you'd see them hanged?

During slavery and beyond, you perfected your machi-nations and tactics. By the time your lying ass sister Carolyn Bryant came on the scene with her false claims about Emmett Till, you had already learned that you could easily get even young Black boys killed. Your tactics in 2020 have evolved but have never really changed. With your regard for truth as irrelevant, you simply need only tell or hint to a white man that you've been wronged in some way. How easy it still is for you *to activate white male rage or violence against Black bodies or Blackness in general.*

You bask in your feigned superiority by instructing, correcting, and abusing Black women. You seek to take from white men the power you think should be yours by manipulating him and playing on his belief that white womanhood should be safeguarded and protected. You collect Black men like tools knowing that the "right" one will do your bidding and then is easily disposable and replaceable. Just like a bus, another one will come along shortly.

Knowing that you never have to get your hands dirty, in your quest for white-man power, you wield your own power by capitalizing on a combination of tropes that involve tears, innocence, fragility, female delicateness, protection and safeguarding of female whiteness, white femininity, womanly wiles, the pedestal, etc.

We see you, white women.

We see you coveting access and entry into the good ole' boys club.

We see you, white women.

We see you not caring about us or our real struggles.

We see you, white women.

We see you clamoring to be acknowledged and recognized for your rightful place alongside white men or above him.

We see you, white women.

We see you actively and complicitly engaging in relegating us to the bottom.

We see you, white women.

We see you enjoying the fruits of privilege at our expense.

We see you, white women.

We see you judging us and viewing us with scorn for the messy choices many of us make just to survive.

We see you, white women.

We see you leaning in and clawing for a better seat at the table.

We see you, white women.

We see you diminishing us for ensuring we can put food on the table.

We see you, white women.

We see you forcing a convenient wedge between us and Black men when you attempt to use us for your white feminist-centered agenda.

We see you, white women.

We see you misunderstanding our feminism that greatly values the safety of our Black husbands, lovers, sons, and brothers at the hands of whiteness.

We. See. You.

It is time for you to also see you.

Read your history. Check the facts. Look at population data. You are the main reason that racism still persists in this country. THE main reason.

Sincerely,
Black women of yesterday and today

Dianne Greyson here, and I'm speaking. I am who I should be. You may not know me but I have a voice. A voice that wants to bring about change, to make a difference, to leave a legacy for my children. I do not want to be tolerated. I want to be respected. Black is the color of my skin and I embrace it.

Karen at a Glance

Karen is the entitled white woman who

does not wear a mask,

cuts in front of us in line,

bumps us in line without an "excuse me,"

demands to speak to our manager,

calls 911 to get us killed,

lies to get her way

manipulates men,

turns on the fake tears when she gets called on her shit.

In short, she is a cunning and devious creature who will stop at nothing to annihilate her adversaries, real or perceived. Though she can't be shamed or canceled, she is prone to fits of rage and crocodile tears both on and off camera—whichever suits her best. Sprinkling her with Holy water won't work. Because she is an assassin trained by whiteness and indoctrinated into whiteness, her tactics are particularly deadly for us. Where the hell did she come from and how in the hell did she grow to be so dangerous? I'm about to tell ya.

The Birth of the Karen

Karen is the archetypal figure of female whiteness that weaponizes whiteness to police us and to manipulate others to harm or kill us. Karen is not a new invention of the Black imagi-nation and has "roots" that go way back to slavery. Karen was even depicted in Alex Haley's *Roots* in the guise of Kizzy's long-time "friend" Missy Ann whose betrayal resulted in Kizzy being sold away from her home and family.

Though the origin of Karen can be traced to slavery and though it is notable that *Roots* depicted a Karen, the official and formalized blueprint for Karen is found in the 1915 silent film *Birth of a Nation,* a film that both depicted the "brutish Black man" who seeks to rape but also depicted the white female body as that which must be protected and safe-guarded. This film is iconic for many reasons that are extremely detrimental to Blackness and Black humanity.

The film can easily be dubbed *The Birth of Karen* because it clearly presumes and establishes white women's status as vulnerable and in need of protection and safeguard from a large, violent, intimidating Black man who intends to rape her. And though the film specifically focuses on the sexual violation of white women, the theme of protection evolved and ex-panded to the white supremacy principle which posits that white women's entire existence and well-being must be pro-tected at all costs.

Additionally, white women have the sacred role of mothers responsible for birthing the white race. They are needed to ensure the continuation of whiteness and dominance so that we "will not replace them" as per the fear chanted 3 years ago by neo-Nazis in Charlottesville bearing phallic tiki-torches.

Post *Birth of a Nation*, Karen made a name for herself long before the term Karen was coined. It's quite laughable that today they continue to be upset over the term and don't realize that it replaced terms like "white witch," "white bitch" "evil white bitch," "cunning bitch," etc.

One of the most dangerous developments in the evolution of Karen (which was epitomized by Central Park Amy Cooper) is how Karen has honed and perfected the biggest tool in her arsenal.

THE LIE.

In the life of Karen, the art of the lie has been a game-changer. The minute Karen realized that she could manipulate white men to believe anything she told them, that was the minute she became a deadly threat. She discovered that she could spin a lie and get us killed. Big fat white lies. And even "small" white lies.

During the period of our enslavement and beyond, white women are known to have lied about being raped by Black men. And because white women know they're regarded as sacred and pure vessels, their word is rarely doubted. The chances that a Black man's word would be regarded over hers? Slim to none. On the contrary, an accusation from a white woman guaranteed no trial and a mob-imposed lynching. It was easy for them to believe and uphold her lie when it aligned with a white worldview.

Not only does Karen not require an actual offense, she also doesn't care if her victims are grown men or children. An equal opportunity liar.

Specifically, think of 14-year-old George Stinney and 14-year-old Emmett Till, but there are many more unknown Black victims who fell prey to the lies of white women. Of course, Emmett Till's encounter with a Karen is likely most familiar to us. Carolyn Bryant's lie is what prompted her husband and her brother-in-law to kidnap, brutally beat, and kill Emmett Till for a transgression that never happened the way she told it. And many years later she, indeed, confessed that she had lied. Yet she has never been held accountable. A classic Karen outcome.

Karen also discovered that she could tell a lie to cover for her own behavior even when—especially when!—her behavior is criminal. Does anyone remember Susan Smith from 1994 who murdered her two young children? She initially told the lie that a Black man had kidnapped her children during a carjacking. She almost got away with it, too. Hmph.

Karen remains a significant enough threat to us to make it into the book's title. Not trump, not MAGAts, not the KKK, not the proud boys, not neo-nazis, not domestic terrorists. All threats, yes. But not like Karen! Karen is in a category all by herself. She has always shown us exactly who she is.

> **Janelle Benjamin** here, and I'm Speaking. I have the blood of warriors who survived the middle passage flowing through my veins. I have God on MY side. Did you not think I would triumph? Silly Karen. I plead the blood of Jesus over you and over all hateful Karens who try to get in the way of Black women's progress at work. You tried it though!

Among our many talents, is our spot-on Karen radar. We can spot them up close, in a voicemail, in an email. We can also sniff out Karen-energy without them saying a word. I remember a few years ago during a trip to New York, I visited my daughter at her work office. She introduced me to some of her colleagues, several of whom were white women. Afterwards, she asked me which of the women was pitted against her. She already knew but was checking if I knew, too. Without skipping a beat, I responded, "The one with the short brown hair nearest the window." Bingo! I was right. When she asked what gave it away, I told her that the white woman's words didn't feel right to me and that she gave off a vibe when she shook my hand.

Karen detector. There should be a job description for that. That feeling and that vibe we get are a gift. Without it, perhaps even more of us would be caught unaware and fall victim to Karen and her schemes. I bet at least 3 out of 4 of us could readily identify the Karen's in our work life without hesitation. And if leadership cared enough to listen to us and take our experiences seriously, we'd produce a list of Karens for them that—if they were to get all of the Karens out of there—it would radically transform the culture.

Workplace Karens, at minimum, are slick and sneaky. At their worst, they are Central Park Amy, who, before she got fired, was likely some Black woman's colleague or manager. The same way that Amy showed her ass in Central Park is the same way Karen operates in the workplace, albeit more subtle and sanctioned, and all too often she reigns from a human resources gate-keeper perch.

Besides Central Park, where are the Karens? In non-profits, in corporate offices, in board offices, in financial institutions, in colleges and universities, in churches, in medical facilities, in government offices, in Zoom meetings, in social media feeds, in mommy groups, in classrooms.

In short, they are e-ver-y-where! Their natural habitat is everywhere. And they will predictably lash out if their whiteness feels threatened in any way.

Having lived through first-hand Karens and the threat and danger they pose, my experiences are exactly the reason I keep that WWW list I told you about earlier – white women to watch. Karen's weaponized whiteness layered with "femininity" makes her a double threat to us and Black men.

Based on how 2020 has already been shaping up, a major Karen event was bound to happen. May 25. Memorial Day. In walks Amy Cooper. Picture it. A Karen with a dog who picked the wrong Black man on the wrong day in the wrong place. Christian Cooper (no relation). A Harvard-educated bird-watcher! He checked all the right whiteness boxes, and it still didn't prevent him from being Karened. Put it like this. If there were to ever be a Black *Gilligan's Island*, Christian Cooper would be the professor. Friendly, smart, resourceful, likeable, non-threatening. She called the cops on the professor!

Amy Cooper was likely not Christian Cooper's first rodeo with a Karen, nor was it our first rodeo watching her in action. What was different this time was the videotaping. Thank goodness he made the decision to continue filming even when she demanded that he stop filming her. Who knows how this would have played out without the videotape evidence to negate the Karen clusterfuck coup she was trying to pull.

Central Park Karen found herself in a bit of a situation. That's what happens when white entitlement and arrogance are reminded that rules apply to them. And oh, the rage and defiance when they are reminded by one of us! The audacity of Christian Cooper to inform her that she's violating park rules. Yes. That was his crime, for which he deserved to die.

So Karen did what she's always done—weaponize her female whiteness to exact punishment on him—and to do it in such a way to not get her own hands dirty. She put on quite the show to assume the out-of-breath, urgent voice of a white female in distress to manipulate male whiteness to swoop in and rescue her from a threatening Black brute. She lied that he was threatening her and her little dog, too (picture the wicked witch of the west crying foul).

In this case, the fact that she didn't call a white husband, partner, or friend but elected to call 911[9] with a lie to get them to immediately send the police betrays her true motive. She didn't simply want Christian Cooper punished; this white bitch wanted him killed! And for what? For politely asking her to leash her dog in accordance with the posted rules of the park. For daring to interrupt her desire to have her dog romp unleashed.

And even with video evidence, even when the jig is up, even when she's busted, this bold Karen decided to pivot with a predictable narrative that would garner victim's sympathy

---

[9] San Francisco passed the CAREN Act in October that makes it illegal to make racially-charged 911 calls.

and support from whiteness. According to her, her life is now ruined. Really?! Let me see if I have this right.

Her attempted murder-by-proxy of a Black man failed.

She was caught.

Now her life is ruined.

Sure, Karen.

> **Erin Jones** here, and I'm speaking. I stand 6' tall. It is INCREDIBLE how often I have been invisiblized - in stores, in meetings. I allowed this for too long. At 40, I made the decision to embrace all of me. I stopped straightening my hair. I now stand 6' with another 5" of colorful Afro. You will see AND hear me. I have much to say.

Karens straight-up pack corporate environments and typically have deep protection unlike their uncouth public Karen counterparts. The workplace is their preferred habitat to carry out their nonsense surreptitiously. And as we know, corporate Karen is known for her cunning, her tears, and her duplicity. All she has to do is drop a word or a comment about one of us, and then before you know it, our relationships with folks get inexplicably weird and then our career mobility takes a free-fall.

Courtesy of workplace Karen, we've been sabotaged, maligned, demoted, written up, reassigned, and fired. Some of us have even trained Karen to become our boss! She remains one of our biggest threats because she wreaks psycho-logical, emotional, and financial damage. In short, Karen can ruin our career. If there were ever a poll conducted on how many of us have willingly left corporate positions in favor of becoming entrepreneurs, the numbers of us who did so in order to escape a Karen would be shocking to only white folks.

In addition to the many dangers that Karens represent, their inability to mind their own damn business is one of the most infuriating! I guess they just can't help their entitled selves after being conditioned to be about the business of policing Black bodies in all public spaces. Policing us has become so normalized that Karens just feel an obligation and a duty to be all up in our bizness. When she can't be the manager, she's calling the manager. And the manager of outdoor spaces is guess who? The police!

I'm envisioning rounding up all "our" Karens in a room and giving them some strategies. I'd first have them stand and give their names and own up to their shit. Picture it.

"Hi. My name is Dawn, and I'm a Karen. I cry to get my boss to side with me against Black women."

Hi. My name is Sharon, and I'm a Karen. I'm a real bitch to Black women when I'm in public....because I can.

Hi. My name is Linda, and I'm a Karen. I got a Black woman fired because she was more qualified than I was.

Now imagine if we could give them some advice... Yeah, I know. I'm being way nicer than they deserve. But stay with me for a minute.

We can call the advice we give them "Self-Cure Remedies for Karens."

1. Mind yo damn bizness.
2. Invest in some kinda "FIT BITch" device to alert you and everybody around you when you're lying (there has to be an app for that).
3. Practice the lost art of "shut the fuck up" (cuz it's not possible to lie and STFU at the same time).
4. Get a damn hobby.

5. Seriously. Get. A. Damn. Hobby.

I'll take one for the team and will happily volunteer to deliver remedy #3.

I need to watch my Karen intake but it's important for us to track these heifers and their actions. They sit at the cusp of white supremacy and faultless white woman privilege. The way they leverage both makes them powerfully dangerous and dangerously powerful.

Public Karen

I guess one might say that cell phones with cameras are mandatory for Black folks so that we can document all interactions with public Karen as well as with police. If we want to piss off Karen, all we need to do is highlight her shrill Karening with our calm voice for contrast. We can also matter-of-factly mention to her that her hair roots have grown out and that her ass looks big in those jogger pants.

And when she screams at the top of her delicate lungs at us to stop videotaping her, we can casually mention that, yeah, the camera really does add 10 pounds. That oughta do it!

KKKaren (A Poem)

KKKaren is who you are
sippin' pinot grigio
with yo' grown-out hair roots
hissin' like a serpent
to draw in men
and do us dirty

KKKaren is who you are
wearin' whiteness like a crown
while your manicured hand
clutches a phone
to call the cops
on our sons and daughters

KKKaren is who you are
layin' claim to all the air
leavin' none for us to breathe
while you curl your tongue
into lies that kill
then demand we forgive

— \o/ tmr

Clear and Present Danger

Sister, you know Karen doesn't need to call the manager when she is "the manager."

One of the newest tricks in Karen's arsenal is "ethnic intimidation," a unique twist to pulling a Karen that I admit I didn't see coming. Thanks to Jillian Wuestenberg, Karens are now returning to their original superpower – turning on the tears. It's part of a triple-play move.

Here's the strategy—

1. claim fear for your life while being the gun-wielding aggressor
2. point to "ethnic intimidation" to justify the behavior
3. turn on the tears and repeat over and over again "I'm not racist"

So, by way of summary – Karen is karening, and the Black family ain't having it, so Karen amps up her karening with a gun, and the Black family still ain't having it. The incident goes viral, and Karen gets a lawyer, and the lawyer is adept at karening and comes up with a defense to excuse the karening as justifiable karening due to "ethnic intimidation" of the Black family.[10] Whut the whut?!

All of this is Karen's attempt to escape responsibility for and consequences of her actions and—I don't want anyone to miss the significance of this part—and also find a way to turn it around and make us responsible for the abuse leveled at us when we dare to call out or push back against the abuse.

White people find it very difficult to de-escalate whiteness, especially if they believe there's been an affront to their whiteness. They are much better at escalating whiteness.

Karens are definitely upping the stakes at the cost of Black lives. This Karen tactic is particularly disturbing because this one got herself all lawyered up. Racism is good about re-inventing itself, and in this case, it seeks to legalize and justify Karen behavior. The irony is not lost on me that she retained male counsel who came up with this brilliantly asinine justification for her pulling a gun on an unarmed family. Oh what charms she must have used to beguile and bewitch!

White Defense of Karen

We all know that white women are triggered by being called Karens and haven't yet figured out that it's a behavior archetype and not a slur like nigger or nigger bitch—pronounced with the harsh and hard "r" and NOT to be mistaken for our

---

[10] "Lawyer for Michigan Couple Who Pulled Gun on Black Family Says They Were Victims of 'Ethnic Intimidation.'" Ishena Robinson. *The Root.* 07/11/2020.

culturally reappropriated "nigga." In a classic clueless twist, they believe that "Karen" and "racist" are the worst names that anybody can ever be called. They betta go on somewhere wit' that.

Well, anyway, I get particularly tickle-annoyed when cis hetero white men get triggered and come to Karen's defense against us "mean ole' Black women."

One of them, like nice racists do when offended by Black folks, came at me with this scolding directive —

"Also—Super minor point but perhaps relevant, and I hesitated to even bring it up—but is there another word you could use besides 'Karen' to refer to that awful person? There are a lot of people named Karen in the world that are not deplorable and super racist like this woman. I think it slightly undermines your position to use the term 'Karen.' I recognize it's become a shorthand in society but maybe WE [emphasis mine] can have a different term."

The absolute caucacity![11] Who the fuck is "we"?! Are you laughing yet or nose-snorting in derision at his paternalistic strategy to teach me? Basically, he's "white virtue signaling."

Important sidenote: He devoted more focus to his visceral reaction to the term Karen than he did to behavior which he described as "deplorable" and "super racist." Let that sink in.

Anyhoo, allow me to translate the whiteness seeping and oozing out from his words:

The term Karen doesn't keep us mildly racist white folks separate from the "deplorable, super racist" white folks. So I

---

[11] Caucacity is the bold audacity of white people who say and do stuff only white people would say and do.

suggest you find a term that keeps us mildly racist white folks protected and comfortable. Things could get unpleasant for you, so I strongly advise another term.

First, as one of my favorite Black political commentators just recently declared in response to white tone-policing, "he can fuck all the way off." Second, what a dumbass. Third, what a dumbass!

He obviously doesn't know a thing about me. That I would kow-tow to a random white man tone-policing my language and offering unsolicited suggestions is beyond the pale (pun intended!). Ugh. What he is doing amounts to corrective measures designed to control me. These measures, when tried with me, never end well---for the perp. Boo, sit down. And shut up.

And at the same time, this kinda shit takes a toll on me. The day-to-day restraint, energy-draining bandwidth, and repe-tition involved in experiencing, explaining, translating, and educating about stuff like this is blaxhausting and an assault on my emotional and mental health.

Kimberly Jones here, and I'm speaking. While working in an environment known for space exploration and engineering wonder, I did my very best to contribute in a positive way. Imagine my surprise when a white female HR VP attempted to admonish me by saying "you always try to be the smartest person in the room." When I am in the room with you I am.

Dissin' Us and Dismissin' Us (A Poem)

dissin' us and dismissin' us
cuz
they programmed to
disparage us
disprove us
dis-count us
discredit us
discourage us

cuz
they know they can't
dis-solve us
disappear us
disillusion us
discern us
dis-spirit us
cuz
we distinct
and un-extinctable

—\o/ tmr

Karen, the Teacher

Forget about the traditional 3R's of school—readin,' writin,' and 'rithmetic. When it comes to the Karens who've been let loose in our children's classrooms, the 3R's are "racism, rules, and roadblocks." These heffahs got their claws on our kids!

Sharla Stevens here, and I'm speaking. It's life or death when Black students don't graduate. At the same time, surviving 12 years of racist schooling kills their spirit. Our schools are conditioned to accept Black failure and fear Black excellence. It's time we created our own schools, on our terms, to protect our youth.

Karen's Son KKKyle

"It is easier to build strong children than to repair broken men."

—Frederick Douglass

Another 2020 surprise. A Texas high school teacher included KKKyle Rittenhouse among a list of individuals for a writing project about a "hero for the modern age." And I can't even say any more, "only in Texas." This is bigger than just Texas. This has always been bigger than just Texas.

Yeah. You read that right. There is no limit to the mass dumbfuckery that is whiteness.

I have questions.

The curious list of figures from the assignment also included Malcolm X, Ghandhi, Cesar Chavez, George Floyd, and Joseph Rosenbaum. You can't make it make sense.

This is just one of many reasons why we continuously lift our voices and protest no matter how draining the daily madness.

Today's school children are being taught by those who would glorify an assault weapon wielding 17-year-old white male who—let's be clear here—would not hesitate to shoot our kids on sight. And then would justify the shooting with the "fear defense." With teachers like this, the schools are sanctioned training camps for ignorance and hate. They're factories for Kyles and Kens, who, unlike Karens that use their womanly wiles as weapons, actually brandish weapons while binding themselves to their 2nd Amendment gun rights.

Homegrown terrorists nurtured in the classroom. And they are still asking us to explain systemic racism because they don't see it! Ha! Hate is being afforded fertile ground in all public spaces. Extremely terrifying and disturbing.

The psychological and emotional safety of our children are already in a precarious state. I can't even imagine being a student today at either the primary, secondary, or college level. My head still can't wrap itself around sitting in even a virtual classroom in 2020 and being given that assignment.

And please don't get me started on the weak non-apology apology released by the school. You know. That performative official statement that gets released when they get caught and their racism gets publicized or televised. So predictable.

And check it out. This one is tone deaf at best.

"An unapproved assignment posted in Google Classroom yesterday has been brought to our attention. Understandably, this caused some concern for the impacted students, and we apologize.

Campus administration immediately removed the unapproved content, and students are not required to complete that assignment.

Due to personnel policies, we are not able to comment further, however, the appropriate steps are being followed pending investigation.

Racial equity is a top priority in Dallas ISD, and we remain committed to providing a robust teaching environment where all students can learn.

It is important that we continue to be culturally sensitive to our diverse populations and provide a space of respect and value. "[12]

Assaults on the psychological and emotional safety are NOT best characterized as "some concern for the impacted students."

I'm tired of these lame apologies that dismiss our pain and trauma. I want to hear apologies that in essence say: "This was an epic mess-up. This teacher was wrong. Full stop. We have taken the immediate measure to pull this teacher out of the classroom. Our main priority is healing for the students and all involved. "

Less word count, more direct, and greater substance. White-washed apologies only make the offense worse and end up widening the circle of dumbassery from the teacher to now the entire school administration.

Seriously, Here They Go!

I'm convinced that something has to be seriously wrong with the way the brain grabs on to and manifests whiteness. Not sure if "cult" accurately captures what we have seen and experienced. There has to be a more deeply embedded psychology. Or maybe it's some next-level white intersectionality that has yet to be formally studied. For real tho, because it's them and not a Tuskegee-brand scientific curiosity, real studies or testing will never be done.

---

[12] "Texas School Assignment Lists Kyle Rittenhouse Among 'Modern Heroes.'" Tom Batchelor. *Newsweek*. 9/17/20.

I wanna know. What the full-on hell is wrong with white people?!

What other people so thoroughly convinces themselves of their superiority and then installs as president the dumbest white man they could find? So dumb that he bragged about acing a dementia test by repeating 5 words in a row!

What other group of people invests in entire whiteness systems that come with racism baked right in and then turn around and claim they feel threatened and fear for their lives?

What other group denies Black children their innocence and childhood and view them as criminals and thugs?

What other group?

What. Other. Group?

I'll wait.

> **Joelle A. Murchison** here, and I'm speaking. But do you hear me? Oh I'm still here; I've claimed my seat. I came to get EVERYTHING my ancestors worked for AND what I deserve. Yes, I hear you – everything you said – and what you didn't say. But it's all good. I am on assignment – on purpose – driven by faith! Get on board or get out my way!

Deadly White Spaces

Every single aspect of Blackness in white spaces has been criminalized—from existing while Black to experiencing mental health episodes.

Insert rules and laws, unspoken and actual.

Now go ahead and insert screaming gun-toting white men, cunning cell-phone carrying Karens, and trigger-happy patty-rollers, and there we have it.

They stay mad!

Karen's Ken

We all know him. He is the self-appointed defender and protector of Karen. And he's dedicated to his self-appointed mission to invalidate and un-verify us all in the service of Karen who doesn't even have to explicitly enlist him to do her bidding.

His attempt at silencing, dismissing, discrediting any threat to her is from the same playbook that requires video as proof that what a Black person says happened, happened.

In his zeal to defend Karen, he shifts the focus onto what we said or did to deserve the Karen treatment we got.

The historical precedent is that during slavery, the verbal or written word of a white person was needed to vouch for a Black person's status as free, to vouch for a Black person occupying certain spaces, etc. Most of what we experience and see today is the modern version of a centuries-old system that is very much alive and well.

The default has typically been to give preferential treatment and validity to white voices that seek to silence us. Ken's M.O. includes

- strategically veiling his hate behind professionalism and a poorly cloaked attempt at reasoning
- dismissing the veracity of scores and scores of anecdotal evidence about Karen
- insisting on quantifiable data to verify others' lived experiences with Karen

- positioning himself as the arbiter and determiner of the credibility of Black voices
- cautioning that this is not the time nor the place to bring up racism
- trafficking in his automatic credibility as a white man defending the honor of a white woman
- virtue-signaling by way of the "lying Black bitch trope" in order to discredit us

Whose Trauma Matters

After George Floyd's murder, 150 Minneapolis police officers filed disability claims for PTSD.[13] What were they traumatized by?

Was it the fact that one of their blue brothers killed George Floyd via a knee pressed into his neck until his breath was snuffed out?

Was it his moaning and crying out for his mother who had already preceded him in death? Did he see her as he stood on the precipice between life and death about to cross over?

Were the officers traumatized by these thoughts?

No.

No to all of this.

They attributed their claims of PTSD to what they have been suffering as a result of the protests arising from George Floyd's murder! Really. Seriously. That's what they all said! It appears that the stress of so many people protesting the murder of a Black body was too much for them.

What I wanna know is where can we file OUR claim.

---

[13] "150 Minneapolis Cops File Disability Claims for PTSD, Which They Attribute to George Floyd Protests." Ishena Robinson. *The Root*. 07/11/2020.

> **Dr. Danyelle Wright** here, and I'm Speaking. After Tony Robinson, I was sad. After George Floyd, I was pissed. After Jacob Blake, I said, "fuck it." I cut out all forms and identities that align to the assimilation due to my oppressor. Starting with my overly processed hair, to my unapologetically Black skin. No more weaves, make-up, and politeness. Just my fist in the air and BLM on my chest.

Meanwhile, Post Traumatic Slave Syndrome (PTSD) coined by Dr. Joy DeGruy has yet to gain the widespread traction it deserves. Dr. DeGruy's work focuses on naming and also affirming the ongoing enduring hurt and injury to Black folks aka 400+ years of generational trauma.

It's 2020, and we still can't seem to reach full consensus that our lives matter, so it's not likely that ongoing trauma to our lives will matter.

Meanwhile the police who kill us are filing claims over their psychological distress due to our protests of them killing us. Sister, no matter how many ways I write it or say it, I can't make it make sense.

Pattyrollers 2.0

Whether walking, running, sleeping, or complying, we're being shot by police. And it has not gone unnoticed by us that Black codes are being (re)activated. "Don't be caught here after dark" and other unspoken laws of Blackness are still very much in effect. Today's pattyrollers just like their pattyroller predecessors, have a duty to police Black bodies and ensure the comfort and safety of white citizenry.

Let me back up with a historical refresher. Slave patrols were the early form of policing in this country because white folks lived in constant fear of rebellions and uprisings. They didn't want our ancestors' dreams and quests for freedom to interfere with their profits and the economic status quo. So the role of the pattyrollers, a name they were given by our ancestors, was pretty basic—control the movements and behaviors of slaves. Sound familiar? Thus, today's police are in essence pattyrollers 2.0.

Anyhoo, according to historian Gary Potter, pattyrollers served three main functions in policing bodies:

1. "to chase down, apprehend, and return [runaway slaves] to their owners"
2. "to provide a form of organized terror to deter slave revolts"
3. "to maintain a form of discipline"[14]

Imposed social control reliant on terror.

At the same time, pattyroller history may be our best shot at understanding their fear. Just as we carry trauma, they carry fear. Fear of us organizing and overthrowing them, similar to the fear of their ancestors who lived in constant panic that our ancestors would rise up and pay back evil for evil. It would certainly explain their assassination of our Black leaders and their attempts to stall any attempts at equity and equality.

They still doing us dirty and fear the blowback.

They know that if we were the kind of people that lived for revenge and payback of the same, there'd be white hell to pay! Instead of a come-to-Jesus reckoning for this country, what

---

[14] "The History of Policing in the United States," Dr. Gary Potter. EKU School of Justice Studies. 06/25/2013.

does whiteness do instead? It doubles down on whiteness and keeps in place law-and-order pattyrollers 2.0 whose role and function remain the same.

They can't very well declare open season on all of us, but they damn sho' can carry out a public killing of any of us on the regular so that we don't forget our place and so we continue to feel terror. Because the role of policing us is such an important one that keeps white society running, pattyroller jobs must be protected and preserved.

In that vein, there are clear steps from the pattyroller "extermination playbook" designed to preserve blue jobs at the cost of Black lives.

- Step 1: Shoot or kill Black body.
- Step 2: Conduct internal investigation that manufactures reasons Black body deserved to be shot or killed
- Step 3: Officially justify shooting or killing
- Step 4: Give generous benefit of the doubt to shooter or killer
- Step 5: Exonerate shooter or killer from responsibility, accountability, and guilt
- Step 6: Repeat step 1

To elaborate a bit more—

The precursor of step 1 is a mindset that views our bodies as armed bodies due to skin color alone. Pattyrollers then approach with a pre-existing "I feel threatened" mentality. They predictably escalate the situation "justifiably" when we do not proffer the "proper" capitulation and deference to whiteness. We saw this with the video of Sandra Bland's traffic stop. Next is arrest and/or shoot and kill.

Anybody who seriously wants to understand why cops are killing us don't have to look far. Today's policing amounts to modern-day slave patrols. Period.

Slave patrols of today and yesterday never cared one iota for preserving our life or keeping us safe. In order to preserve a life and keep it safe, you have to first believe you see a life!

At best they see 3/5 human. At worst they see property they still think they own.

Law enforcement in this country is an inherently racist system. Police are tasked with maintaining "law and order"— a dog-whistle phrase popularized in the 60's and well into the 80's.

And firing racist cops does nothing to address the system. The same as firing a racist CEO or voting out a racist president does nothing to address the underlying system that allows racism to thrive.

Firing that one or few bad apples serves to fire that one or few bad apples. And I can't even with those folks who want everybody to applaud the good cops while doing nothing to acknowledge and take action to stop the killings. While they busy clappin.' we gettin' shot and killed.

The system itself is the rot. There's been no real police reform. Why? Think about that. Police are central to a "police state" designed to uphold white supremacy.

The policing of, terrorizing of, and killing of black bodies will continue until the entire anti-Black system is dismantled. Police will continue to kill us and be rewarded with paid administrative leave followed by exoneration and reinstatement or be fired and eligible for transfer to another county's police department to resume their "law-and-order" reign of racial terror.

The status quo is what's killing us. Sanctioned racism is what's killing us. Let us each understand how deathly lethal it is when Karen teams up with police!

Police and white civilians alike can easily manufacture just cause. Again, take the "I feel threatened" defense and justification, for example. It's only for white folks. It's a cover for killing us. White feelings—real or manufactured—mean more than Black lives. Always have.

Meanwhile, we feel threatened daily. We feel unsafe daily. That we feel this way is a deliberate feature of the system. Fear and terror tactics initially used during slavery never went away. The tactics just evolved. Think Reconstruction era, Jim Crow era, Civil Rights era.

The system spawns thousands and thousands of patty-rollers just like Derek Chavin, the killer of George Floyd.

Who in his life made him turn that corner of hate? Is his mother a Karen who suckled him from infancy on hate and trained him up in it?

Where did his main influences come from? Who were his neighborhood friends, teachers, and coaches? How did they influence him?

When did something inside him fundamentally change? When did he surrender himself to a cancerous hate that would culminate in him single-handedly and cold-bloodedly pressing the breath of life from another human being?

How did he remain calm for 8 minutes and 46 seconds and not realize that his soul was on the line? If George Floyd was looking at the face of Jesus and his mother, what face was Derek Chauvin looking upon as he casually and calmly killed?

What a legacy he now has—forever known as the cop who killed George Floyd on camera for the whole world to watch. We each saw him adorned in the uniform of a job that required an oath to protect and serve. Pretty pathetic! And so is the oath. The quiet part out loud is understood as "protect and serve whiteness and white folks."

But wait, I can't stop thinking about this Chauvin dude. And it may be partly because I saw a picture of him as a little boy. I've been wracking my brain trying to figure out what the hell happened to him.

Let me go back in time for a moment and think about his parents, who I'm sure loved him. His cold-heartedness was not his beginning. He wasn't born with hate. None of us is born with hate. There's no mistaking though that cold-hearted cruelty is where he ended up. Somebody or something taught him that.

I wonder what his parents taught him, what values they instilled in him. Were they the ones who taught him to hate?

I wonder these things because I want white parents to teach their children to not grow up and kill ours. It's easier to prevent the creation of a killer than to fix one already created.

Everybody knows the importance of the "be kind to others" talk and the "sex talk." How 'bout the "good" white folks start prioritizing the "race talk"?

The 1619 Project gives me hope, but we'll see because that whole project has been attacked for being "divisive." And we all know what divisive means.

Yeah, I know. I'm off on a tangent.

I'm not okay.

Pattyrollers Gon' Getcha (A Poem)

Pattyrollers gon' getcha
Wit' they blue hoods

Pattyrollers gon' getcha
Wit' they badge to kill

Pattyrollers gon' getcha
Wit' they iron ropes

Pattyrollers gon' getcha
Wit' they tobaccy chewin' sneer

Pattyrollers gon' getcha
Wit' "gal" and "boy" on their lips

Pattyrollers gon' getcha
Wit' "nigger" in they heart

Pattyrollers gon' getcha
Wit' they search for freedom papers

Pattyrollers gon' getcha
Wit' they knock n' kill warrants

Pattyrollers gon' getcha
Wit' they motorized slave chasers

Pattyrollers gon' getcha
Wit' they bullets in our back

Pattyrollers gon' getcha
Wit' they knee on our neck

Pattyrollers gon' getcha
Pattyrollers done gotcha

— \o/ tmr

Asylum Ain't Just for Black Men

"U.S. Black Men Could Seek Asylum." That's what the headline said. Nothing about Black women. We were mysteriously missing from making a big splash in the news. Did you even know?

In summary, "...the United Nations Human Rights Council surveyed racial discrimination and police brutality in the United States" and determined that police brutality "...has come to symbolize the systemic racism causing PERVASIVE, DAILY, LIFELONG, GENERATIONAL, and too often LETHAL HARM [emphasis mine]. This suggests that African American men have such a 'well-founded fear of persecution' that they could be eligible for asylum in other countries."[15]

I've provided this asylum information for every anti-racism and DEI training I've led since the news came out. When I share the news, I follow up with the question, "How many of you are aware of this?" Nobody has yet to raise their hand.

I also ask the question, "How many of you are surprised that Black women are not included? Again no hands go up. White folks don't think about us like that.

When it comes to the Black community, it remains a historical fact that Black straight men are the privileged ones[16] of anti-Black racism. Not Black LGBTQIA+. And certainly not Black women.

Black straight men are the ones who garner the primary focus and attention as targets of anti-Black racism. Black straight men are the ones whose killings by police can galvanize entire communities in protest. Black women's killings

---

[15] "U.S. Black Men Could Seek Asylum." Leila Morsey. *New York Daily News*. 07/20/2020.

[16] Yeah, I know. I'm deliberately employing a non-standard use of a familiar term.

don't do that in the same way. Even BLM, founded by three Black women, has come to be associated with Black men.

The abuses and killings of Black women have never garnered the same priority. All one has to do is compare the reactions to Breonna Taylor's killing to those of Ahmaud Arbery and George Floyd.

Yes, this recent asylum-eligible declaration is good news for its recognition and acknowledgement of the seriousness of anti-Black racism for Black men. That the organization didn't include Black women sends the message that what Black women face under the same system is not dire and not life-threatening. And this couldn't be further from the truth. That society does not fight hard enough for Black women is closer to the truth.

So, my comment generally on the declaration is this: The U.S. is in a state of free fall. And the fall is more epic than the fall of Rome. White supremacy, hate, capitalism, hubris, etc.— all of it has never been a good look. The optics are down-right embarrassing but at the same time, since 2016, it's right on brand.

That we assess levels of bad is quite chilling. We don't think about a good place to live or a bad place to live. It's really about what's bad, more bad, less bad. Just like presidential elections—what's the lesser of two evils? What candidate won't incite people to kill us? Same thing with evaluating places to live. What place is the least unsafe or the least racist?

This would be quite the news for folks like Nina Simone, James Baldwin, Josephine Baker, and others who opted to leave this country during their lifetime in order to give themselves some racial rest.

Sharon Hurley Hall here, and I'm speaking. I don't have the privilege of overlooking the fact that so many countries were built on—and grew rich on—Black people's enslaved labor, yet we still aren't truly free, and have never received compensation. Though, I ask you, what could really compensate for being trafficked, enslaved, discriminated against, despised, deprived and hated?

Karen's Collection of Black Tools[17]

This species of Karen poses a unique kind of threat. She's not calling the police on us nor is she actively sabotaging us in the workplace. This Karen is the one who shouts from the rooftop that she is "woke" and anti-racist. She is also known to condemn Karens without realizing she is one. Her feelings, her ego, and her thirst for power and influence wilfully blind her to what and who she is.

Consider Sandra, for example, who fits the profile. She's established herself as a racial equity and justice advocate, albeit fake. She's really a champion for white women and only throws in the racial stuff for appearances. She says just enough to fool white folks and a fair amount of Black folks about her racial consciousness. Instead of amplifying the voices of Black folks, she opts to speak about us, for us, without us.

The fake ally stance provides this type of Karen with the perfect cover to advance her own agenda and keep herself centered. Centering reinforces her white dominance. She does

---

[17] Yeah, I said it. Black tools. It's either tools or fools. You choose.

this by collecting gullible and clueless Black men who fall for her charms and her damsel in distress routine. She takes advantage of their disenfranchisement and lures them in with her feigned acceptance of their Blackness. And they in turn are suckered by the welcome and jump at the chance to align with her. Just as it is the case that 45 has a slew of enablers, the same can be said for this Karen. She keeps more than one in her collection. Tools are disposable and wear out their usefulness, so she keeps several.

Like moths drawn to a flame, Black men are at her beck-and-call. This makes all Karens at minimum a double threat. One, they activate white men into serving as enforcers of the white code. Two, they dispatch Black men to defend them and shut others down whom they perceive to be a threat—real or perceived.

She is your high-level Karen variety. This one is an expert at exploiting the sympathy of Black men and holds court over them with the power of whiteness coupled with white feminism. Lethal combination.

So what's her main game? Securing power. Cloaking behind a fake commitment to racial equity and justice, she gets off on challenging white men's power and shutting down Black women who see right through her mess. When Karen is triggered by accusations that she's racist, corrections to her assertions, or challenges to her intentions, she's quick to pivot to her own oppression as a woman. She also enlists Black men to go to bat for her. How do I know? I've been on the receiving end of this particular species of Karen several times.

She spouts beliefs and claims about her "racial wokeness" as a cover for what she really cares about—advancing white feminism. And we all know that white feminists ain't never cared about the concerns of Black women or non-Black women of color. She keeps making it clear with each voting cycle that securing her place at the top of the whiteness chain is her end-game.

Due to who she is and what she says, this Karen frequently elicits negative responses from white men who are die-hard whiteness but with a heavy dose of patriarchy. This is where her Black tools come in, the ones who fall for her claims of "allyship" and who've heard her performative words defending and supporting the Black community. All she needs to do is drop their name and they come running to defend her against the bad white men.

Karen also frequently elicits corrections from Black women who take legitimate issue with her claims, thus outing her as a "false anti-racist prophet." Instead of responding to the valid claims raised by Black women, this Karen cues up the violin music for her "poor me" centering.

"I don't understand why Black women don't see that I'm pushing for the same things they are." (LIE)

"I don't see how Black women could misinterpret my comment the way they did." (GASLIGHTING)

"Instead of your being divisive, I want us to come together as sisters." (GASLIGHTING PLUS LIE)

And yes, she actually went there with that "sisters" crap! Sisters?! Hmph. There she go with that "we share a womanly bond" ploy that white women use to disarm us. It's a lie. She no more believes it than we do. She's establishing that she's the reasonable one and that, of course, Black women are the unreasonable ones. Cue my eye-roll. Besides, she insists that white men are the worst and that she's on our side. She pretty much goes all-in on her white woman show.

And though the sister tactic is particularly offensive, it's especially effective for Black tools that she aims to draw out.

These would be the Black men who agree that we should stand with our "white sisters" and who gladly jump in to take Karen's side against us. Ugh. This manipulative Karen can seem dainty and delicate on a moment's notice and have Black men eating out of her hand—the same hand she'd use to call the cops on their asses in a heartbeat!

When Karen realizes that we're not budging or walking back anything we said, her true colors surface in bold display. Conveniently forgetting and abandoning her sister philosophy, she embarks on a mission to destroy us. This usually involves a campaign to paint herself as the victim of an angry Black woman, to slander and defame our reputation, and to brag about and cite all the Black men who agreed with her.

Did you notice another distinguishing characteristic of this Karen? She does not apologize. That's because this species of Karen is never wrong. Only those who disagree with her are wrong. Only those who don't support her are wrong.

Tompromised™[18]

Our 13% in this country are so scattered, so divided, and so traumatized that some of us fall prey to the lure of whiteness. There are way too many of us chasing white acceptance versus valuing Black empowerment. How many of us is too many? One. Yes, even one.

The stakes are too high to make Blackness—that subscribes to whiteness—comfortable. Too much is at stake for us to keep telling each other that we understand why some Black folks made the choice they made and why they let themselves be

---

[18] Please note that the Uncle Tom of Harriet Beecher Stowe's 1852 novel, *Uncle Tom's Cabin*, is a martyr and not a sell-out. It wasn't until 1919 that the term became an insult in response to various forces of the changing sociopolitical landscape.

used to enact harm against us that serves the interest of whiteness.

So, nah. This ain't that.

We can't all the time be telling white folks about their shit without dealing with our own shit, too. So, gurl, pull up a chair and hold on…

Let me turn the mic over to Dr. Kimya Nuru Dennis to drop a word to us.

Dear Black women,

There's a need for us to draw a clearer line between our goals and our behaving in a manner comforting to white people. Whether for acceptance, for labels such as "kind" and "professional" based on white standards, or for profit, Black women must have more dealbreakers in our personal lives and professional lives. Being mentally and physically exhausted will only continue if we consider it a compliment when called "strong Black woman" in Black families, during election times, and as it pertains to mental and emotional capacity to handle life stressors.

This contributes to the prevalence of us doing unpaid labor and underpaid labor. Once we realize how much other people are paid to do the same work and even less work, we realize that our work is essentially being stolen, put in a different package, and used to profit white people, Brown people, and Black men. We are not being properly cited, given credit, and paid for our work. Further, this abuse of Black women is also done by other Black women, all to accommodate and assimilate white dominant areas that are welcoming to anyone willing to speak and behave in ways comforting to white people.

Black women claim to be exhausted while contributing to the problematic system that is harmful and exhausting. Is there a such thing as consensual blaxhaustion? If there is, are Black people, specifically Black women, to blame for our circumstances? If there is not such a thing as consensual blaxhaustion, what needs to be done to reduce the tendency for Black people to appease white people and appease anti-Black Brown people?

Blame them, yes. However, it's not enough to blame white people including white women—who are the same white dominance as white men. It is not enough to blame anti-Black Brown people for focusing on comforting white people. It is important for Black people to be honest that too many Black people are celebrating being tokens and selling out to white people for the purpose of white acceptance and white profit. It is not acceptable to tokenize for profit and then declare oneself a victim of white abuse.

Sincerely,
Dr. Kimya Nuru Dennis
Activist, Sociologist, and Criminologist

There are two types of tompromised Black folk: unconsciously tompromised and consciously tompromised. Generally speaking, Karen's tools fall into the former category. Whether willing or unwilling participants in our own oppression, tompromised folks remain a threat preventing us from truly mobilizing and uniting ourselves to "play offense" to secure our best interests. Instead, we've relegated ourselves to settling to "play defense" against active threats. Reactive instead of proactive.

Type 1. Unconsciously tompromised. Many of us fall into this category and only recognize it in retrospect once we've unlearned our own internalized whiteness and conditioned self-hatred. These are the ones of us who are looking but not seeing. The ones of us seeing but not discerning. The ones of us hearing but not understanding. The ones of us talking but not really saying anything. The ones of us active but not activated.

It's when we operate on what we don't know we don't know. And that by itself makes us easily influenced and easily used.

These are the ones of us that Malcolm X would be shouting at to WAKE UP, "you're being bamboozled." The danger with being unconsciously tompromised is that if it isn't caught and treated, it can advance to something more sinister.

The name Herman Cain comes to mind as an extreme example of what it looks like when the unconscious becomes conscious and instead of remedying it, the person embraces it. Cain is also a stark commentary of the times—a prominent casualty of both the 'Rona and racism. His latter-day courting and cavorting with whiteness proved fatal, another tragic and more shameful footnote to add to his life. And how did whiteness reward his loyalty? It barely acknowledged his death and marched on. Just another disposable Black life.

Type 2. Consciously tompromised. These are the ones who purposely and deliberately set out to accommodate and pacify whiteness and actively betray their own Blackness. They even attempt to silence those of us who choose to fight for racial equity and justice, who call out whiteness, and who express our pain and rage over our oppression.

Like unconsciously tompromised folks, consciously tompromised folks come in all varieties. Among several stand-out figures is Candace Owens, widely regarded as an opportunist with views widely regarded as objectionable and damaging to the majority of us.

Folks in the consciously tompromised category are driven by white acceptance, white benefits, and profit. They are easily recognizable based on the following characteristics:

- they publicly go against us
- they publicly side with whiteness against us
- they go against Black progress
- they put forth a view known to be popular with whiteness and unpopular with Blackness for the sole purpose of getting in good with whiteness
- they deny the extent of racism's impact
- they align themselves with white influencers
- their run is usually limited when whiteness finds them no longer useful
- their only true loyalty is to themselves and their own best interests
- they turn on a dime
- they willingly harm us at the bidding of whiteness
- they publicly fawn over and praise white folks
- they are for sale

White folks will usually hold up these Black folks as model Black folks and even point us to them as a way of teaching us or correcting us. These folks are also promoted, advanced, sponsored, or given a platform. They in effect, have sold their souls to do the dirty work of whiteness. Why? Again, they are operating for their own benefit and for what they can gain. And they don't hesitate to throw us under the bus in the process.

However, their run is usually limited when whiteness finds them no longer useful. Cuz with whiteness, Black folks who cross over to the white side are too much and never enough.

Black folks' desire for fulfillment and satisfaction based on massa's paradigm never ends well. History bears out the disastrous consequences. One need only look to the period of our enslavement to trace how white folks encouraged and rewarded "sell-out" behavior. It never got the tompromised anywhere, and never got them long-term or permanent benefits. Why? Because whiteness ALWAYS sees and knows Blackness as less than. And tompromised folks are foolish to believe otherwise. No matter what lengths Blackness goes to, this basic enduring rule of whiteness has stood firm.

No matter how much white ass Blackness kisses.

No matter the excuses that Blackness has offered on behalf of whiteness.

No matter the Black lives that Blackness is willing to shit on.[19]

As Angela Davis so famously stated, "If they come for me in the morning, they will come for you in the night."

Tick. Tock.

A Tale of Two Presidents

There were only two qualifications that the current squatter in the big house needed for the presidency. Just two. Possession of whiteness and a penis. Performance was secondary at best. And according to Stormy Daniels, the performance of the latter qualification is questionable. He is an insecure, inadequate, little man in the country's biggest job. Plus he's white and racist, which makes him dangerous.

The brand of whiteness that gives the current big house occupant his appeal has been his ability to give voice to all the ugliness and evil that lurks underneath the white American

---

[19] Whiteness by proxy can be just as detrimental to one's finances, career, emotions, mental state, etc.

Dream. His platform was built on hate for and resentment over the 8 years of Obama's presidency. And when he assumed office, his policies involved affirming and stoking that hate coupled with actively deconstructing Obama's policies.

Folks like to say that 45 is "unfit" for office and that he lacks strength of character. I disagree. He is exactly the fit and strength of racist character needed. What he represents is a reminder and radical shift and return to "Make America Great Again" with an understood "Make America White Again" overtone because America was never great.

Trump's America lies in the part of the U.S. Constitution that declared us as 3/5 of a person. The film *Birth of a Nation*, in addition to its conveyance of the importance of safeguarding white womanhood, was filled with all kinds of blatant nods to the KKK. On top of that, President Woodrow Wilson screened the film in the big house! That's the equivalent of a presidential endorsement. So, yeah, 45 is uniquely suited and fit for the office so that this country can be returned to its "original factory settings." We also owe him and his followers a debt of gratitude for putting a worldwide end to that whole master race thingy. 45 is evidence that stupid and powerful can co-exist in the same entity.

In stark contrast, Obama and his family had to be damn near perfect. Think about the Black girl tax on steroids. They had to be way more than twice as good in every space they occupied, including "at home" in the big house. Just think about all the times that white folks must have called him and his entire family "uppity." Easily several times a day.

With Obama, there was not one scandal of him grabbing pussies or paying off porn stars. His biggest scandals included wearing a tan suit and biking while wearing a helmet. That's the kind of stupid racist hypocrisy that flows from whiteness. And because every single one of us knows what it's like to live while Black, we know that it must have been absolute racist hell for Obama, Michelle, and their daughters for 8 years. And to do it with the grace and dignity that each of us knows can be so very hard to summon and keep turned on!

To this day, four years after he left office, I like to imagine what he and Michelle's private conversations must have been like. In those private moments of safety when they could say what they really wanted to say, I wonder what they said?

Obama: "Can you believe these racist muthafuckas?!"
Michelle: "I know, right?! And their idiot-ass men are almost just as bad!"

I don't know about you, but that's how I envision it. With our sistahQueen Michelle on the same page as us about who poses the relative greater danger!

> **Tameca Miles** here, and I'm speaking. So you would prefer to listen to zombie-acting white people and nonproductive brown-nosing MF rather than receive these quality results? Cause they don't like me? Listen... Jesus performed miracles while people planned to crucify Him. Harriet Tubman led people to freedom despite their fears and bounty for her head. We the same. Back up. I got work to do!

White Women, these 4 Years Are on You

The data backs me up. Black women gathered up our momentum and headed out to the polls in full force in 2016 to try and ensure this menace would not get elected. Because we

125

knew. Black women always know...things. If everybody would vote the way Black women vote, we wouldn't be in this mess. And oh, it was already a mess, but we knew this racist mediocre white man would make it much worse. And we weren't wrong.

And now we discover that white women pulled the same shit for 2020, and at a higher number than 2016! Elections haven't *determined* who white women are; rather, elections have *revealed* who they've always been.

Anyhoo, we turned out in full force in 2016 only to find out that we had been betrayed once again by white women who prize their whiteness over any kind of professed sisterhood or commitment to equity and equality. What woman in her right mind, with or without daughters, votes for a man who brags about grabbing women's pussy and has a multitude of believable sexual assault allegations against him?!?

The events of 2016 further strengthened my resolve around why I insist on keeping a WWW list – white women to watch. My resolve has been growing steadily stronger since – based on their subsequent silence, their subsequent lock-step with their white men, and their prioritization of whiteness. Based on MY experiences, both direct and indirect, white women as a group are not my sisters. Sure, there are few here and there, who have proven themselves as accomplices, but in terms of turning out for us in numbers, nah. White women ain't never been in it for us. They are about chasing what white men have and collecting and using enough unwitting Black tools to help them get it. Period.

When Was America Great? (A Poem)

when was America great
was it when this land was "discovered"
was it when this land was stolen
was it when this land was "settled"
was it when First Peoples were killed
was it when First Peoples were rounded up
was it when First Peoples walked the trail of tears

when was America great
was it when Black bodies were snatched
was it when Black bodies were chained
was it when Black bodies were sold
was it when Black bodies were branded
was it when Black bodies were hanged
was it when Black women were raped

when was America great
was it when Black bodies were three-fifths
was it when Black bodies were denied the vote
was it when Black children were spat on
was it when Black bodies sat at the back of the bus
was it when Black leaders were gunned down
was it when Black bodies pleaded "don't shoot"

when was America great
when

— \o/ tmr

ACT III

Coronaviracism™: A Tale of Two Pandemics

The 'Rona Ain't Racist: Some of Its Closest Friends Are Black (A Poem)

the 'Rona don't see color
it sees just human hosts
the 'Rona believes all lives matter
not just the Black ones

the 'Rona don't have a racist strand
it loves the masked and unmasked
the 'Rona ain't privileged
it thrives high and low

the 'Rona don't stereotype
it strikes in and out the margins
the 'Rona don't discriminate
it deals in equal opportunity death

— \o/ tmr

My Personal Battle with Fear of the 'Rona

The 'Rona has been doing just as much revealing as it's doing causing. In the early days of this coronavirus era, my OCD and anxiety were more exposed and exacerbated than in BC times (before coronavirus). A week or more can go by without my stepping outside my home. I've come to terms with that relative to managing through the alternative.

One of the alternatives involves going for walks outside with my husband. For each person approaching us on the sidewalk, I obsessed on whether they'd be as serious about the 6 ft of distancing as I. I obsessed on if they had a plan A and a Plan B. I obsessed over whether they were familiar with sidewalk etiquette. I obsessed over obsessing.

My brain typically moves way faster than I walk, so you can imagine how taxing this all was. Do I head to the grass and risk stepping in dog shit (which means throwing away my shoes on the spot and walking barefoot cuz I don't keep shoes soiled with dog shit)? Or do I head into the street and trust cars will avoid hitting me? Are runners breathing through their mouths and depositing moisture droplets in the air? Will sweat droplets fly onto me? Needless to say, walking outside hasn't been good for my well-being. The mental strain greatly over-shadows the physical benefits.

It was four months after the March shutdown that I ventured out in July for my inaugural trip to the grocery store. In the early days, I sent my husband out for groceries because my anxiety was too high for me to manage.

My trips outside and my trips to the grocery store remain very limited. I suffer from anxiety and panic attacks. My expectation is that businesses will adhere to and enforce their own posted policies that everyone entering their establish-ment must wear a mask. Where I live in Texas, they rarely make good on this and as far as I'm concerned, they've violated their contract with me when I see people walking around without wearing a mask.

Anxiety is not new for me. Until now, I've been able to manage it, and, to a large degree, hide it from those outside of my immediate family. Like everything in its path, coronavirus has exposed and magnified all of it. My anxiety, and also my panic, my fears, my insecurities. What hasn't been helpful are the folks with good intentions and unsolicited advice who may or may not be faith-based that preach to me about how I should feel or not feel. That hasn't been helpful and has further contributed to my overall state of un-okayness.

When 'Rona Met Racism

Sad. Sobering. Surreal. We are collectively grappling with coronavirus stress disorder (CVSD)—grief, anxiety, fear, depression, isolation, loneliness—in addition to the racism we've always been grappling with.

Coronaviracism.

The term captures the dual forces of two pandemics. Specifically in 2020, this country is primarily characterized by covid19 and anti-Black racism, which is different than "regular" racism.

> **Leah Slater-Radway** here, and I'm speaking. For many non-Blacks, 2020 was a great catalyst of change - an annoyingly loud alarm clock jolting them awake to our reality. For us, it was repetition. From now on, non-Blacks must walk beyond the realms of words through to allyship (not the performative kind) and finally to advocacy. Only then will we reach the destination of equality, inclusion and belonging.

And—a big AND—the early reports support that we are the ones contracting and dying from the 'Rona at higher rates. Think about it. It makes sense from a racism standpoint. We have less access to testing which stems from serious inequities in healthcare to begin with. We are more likely to have preexisting conditions that make us more likely to succumb to the virus because again...racial inequities, lack of access to healthcare, etc. We are also more vulnerable to the biases of medical personnel and are likely to not have our symptoms be taken seriously.

Coronaviracism™: A Tale of Two Pandemics

"Thanks" to the 'Rona, more than 20 cities and counties have now declared racism a public health crisis. It appears that some folks are just now realizing that being Black was a health hazard long before covid19. We've been tellin' em this stuff for years.

In short, covid has illuminated racially disparate outcomes not just in heath and healthcare, but also in life expectancy, income, housing, wealth, education, employment, incarceration, etc. No longer can there be denial of and hiding from systemic racism. Black and brown communities continue to be impacted. In stark contrast, white folks went berserk over not being able to get a haircut and go out for a drink. I coined the term coronaviracism due to the intersection of the virus and racism. The former lays bare and exposes the latter.

Coronaviracism can be both a consciously sought-out outcome and an inadvertent consequence of existing racism. Coronaviracism happens when those in power knowingly allow, leverage, and weaponize public health conditions that disproportionately impact us by subjecting us to circumstances in which our very life becomes even more marginalized and threatened.

The (Dis)United States is THE epicenter of both pandemics—coronavirus and racism. And, lo and behold, both pandemics have exposed this country's ugly underbelly.

- existing power structures are fueled and supported by racism
- narratives are controlled by those in power
- insufficient care and regard are reserved for the most vulnerable citizens
- work which we were told couldn't be done remotely can indeed be done remotely

- disabled individuals could've been working from home instead of being faced with inadequate accommodations or with unemployment
- some companies only do the right thing when forced or compelled
- profit is ALWAYS king
- people hold a universal shared fear of running out of toilet paper (I'm still trying to understand this one)

Cruel, life-threatening and life-ending proof is everywhere. Who knew it would take a virus to expose how racism permeates EVERYTHING. Our voices, our pain, the existing data have never been enough.

Yet and still, it took the ravages of covid, massive deaths, widespread record unemployment, a videotaped Amy Cooper (pronounced Karen), and back-to-back killings of the most recent black bodies we know about: Ahmaud Arbery, Sean Bell, Breonna Taylor, Manuel Ellis, George Floyd, etc.

And as we race (pun intended) to create a vaccine for covid, why haven't we yet to apply that same urgency to the worldwide racism pandemic? Eye-roll, y'all. It's only a rhetorical question.

Until that time arrives, covid experts have their testing and contact tracing methods. When it comes to racism, I have mine.

Also, wouldn't it be something if fighting racism were a priority of those in power? Again, rhetorical question.

His and Her Carriers of the Racism Infection

HIM.

We know he's infected when his temperature gets elevated during times when whiteness is decentered and Blackness is centered. We know he's infected when his skin gets thinner and his breathing grows more "fragile" in response to any efforts aimed at equity, equality, inclusion, or fairness.

And typically he betrays himself as infectious at a dangerously toxic level with bouts of anger and rage at the unfairness of it all for him and his kind. In keeping with coronavirus protocols, he needs to be rounded up and self-quarantined immediately and indefinitely until a cure is developed. I have it on white authority that "caging" is an effective remedy for containing people. In this situation, caging is based on a need to flatten the curve and mitigate the risk that more and more of us might be harassed, targeted, and killed by the infected. Plus, there's a small chance that the infection rate might be slowed down, thus preventing new infections.

HER.

When she is infected, she usually presents differently albeit with greater threat and danger. Her signs of infection can be harder to detect due to fake ally behaviors. She will often present with a case of the vapors, feigned sensibilities, duplicitous tongue, cell-phone 911 trigger fingers, and those infamous crocodile tears.

Most times though she will show no obvious symptoms and operates as a cunning and witting carrier and proxy for the infection. Additional measures beyond social distancing are required for her as she is known to utilize both direct and indirect methods of transmitting. Vigilance coupled with a "girl, bye" delivered Black woman style can be a short-term treatment but not a cure.

As with him, the importance of containing the infection and limiting the spread is key in finally getting the infection under control for the first time.

This Just Stinks to High Hell

Well, the 'Rona and racism wanted company, and so who did they invite? Pollution.

"Across the US, black people are dying from Covid-19 at disproportionately high rates. While there are many different factors at play behind the stark racial disparities—there's one possible reason that's been lurking in the air for decades: pollution. Decades of segregation and housing discrimination have put black Americans at greater risk of living near chemical plants, factories and highways, exposing them to higher levels of air pollutants. These pollutants have had a chronically negative impact on health, leading to conditions like hypertension and asthma. Now, those same diseases are associated with more severe cases of Covid-19."[20]

And if this isn't enough all by itself, the "party" gets bigger in an area of Louisiana called "Cancer Alley." The history of environmental injustice based on the intersection of race, ethnicity, and socioeconomic status is no secret. Hell, in 2020, Flint still doesn't have clean drinking water.

Land that has been overprocessed, doesn't grow anything, and is in the middle of nowhere is where we'll find the "BIPOC us" that fit "the description" of 'Rona victims.

The Environmental Protection Agency (EPA) is yet another joke, always rolling back protections and catering to big business. Its self-described misnomer of "protection" adds insult to injury. Fuck the EPA. Cuz they're killing us, too. EPA.

---

[20] "One Reason Why Coronavirus Is Hitting Black Americans the Hardest." Ranjani Chakraborty. vox.com. 05/22/2020.

Hmph. Environmental *profit* agency is more like it. Yeah, let's go with that.

The Emergency of White Inconvenience

Even the word essential took on new meaning this year. For a moment, folks who had typically been relegated to the bottom through a combination of race and class were having a bit of a moment because of an arbitrary "essential designation." The irony wasn't lost on us.

Thanks to the 'Rona, low-wage work and unskilled work quickly received a semantics makeover. The work is considered essential. The workers also got a semantics makeover. Essential disposable workers. But nobody is saying that quiet second part out loud. So they're being hailed as essential workers.

Essential workers have always been the ones keeping society running. Grocery workers, sanitation workers, mail and package carriers, public transit folks, etc. Prior to now, they were made to feel invisible and unimportant rather than essential, even though they have always labored to keep society running, making it possible for all of us to meet our basic needs.

At the same time, they've lacked access to benefits like paid leave and health insurance, and many of their employers aren't providing sufficient protective equipment, such as masks and gloves.

Many of them are Black and calling them heroes or thanking them is not enough. They need to be paid a fair livable wage. They need paid leave and health insurance. They need PPE.

Regard for people is not at the center of tackling the 'Rona, which aligns with what we know already. The 'Rona lays bare and amplifies the ugliness of business, government, and society which I call "The P Principle." The P Principle prioritizes all else over people. This includes

profit
power
politics
policy
privilege
process
procedure

> **Sibyl Biggers** here, and I'm speaking. We see WHAT you are. Our bodies are no longer free capital. Focus on minding your own family and business. We will continue to teach and build our families, businesses, communities and change nations with our knowledge and culture—like our ancestors from whom we descended. Fulfilling our true legacy, that your oppression attempted to suffocate. Bye bigot, bye.

The outcries and worry over 401K during covid are not coming from a homeless population of over half a million. Perhaps the homeless are more concerned about how they're going to adhere to the rules of social distancing and the recommended frequency of hand-washing. Perhaps they're more focused on NOT DYING.

And I can't seem to recall that all essential workers who are being forced into returning to work are receiving paid sick leave benefits.

And oh, I can't remember a time when leadership chose to forego profit rather than risk even one lost life.

Check out Disney, the "happiest place on earth," where paying customers are called guests, and employees are called cast members. Hmph. Disney leadership got tired of losing money and decided, "Fuck it. The park's open. Bring yo' kids. Bring yo' friends. We infectin' ev'rybody."

What I do notice is how quick to act are those of power and privilege when they and their interests face an existential threat. And yet, long before coronavirus hit, we and other members of marginalized groups had been living and still are living under existential threat EVERY. SINGLE. DAY. We are greatly and disproportionately impacted.

As much as we would like the anthem to be "stronger together" or "we'll get through this together," the reality is that this country has never made good on that "together" part. For starters, "together" should've always included fair labor policies and healthcare for everyone. Whose brilliant idea was it to tie employment to healthcare? Gross inequality, coupled with widespread unemployment, has proven to be unsustainable. Hmph. We tried to tell 'em.

Meanwhile, Jeff Bezos, Bill Gates, Mark Zuckerberg, Elon Musk, and Bernard Arnault have amassed fortunes exceeding $100 billion—during a year of dire financial crises for so many. Many folks are in food lines for the first time in their lives. Let all of this sink in. Now look back at the list of five men and guess what they all have in common. At least for five people, the year 2020 has been a banner year for increasing net worth. Because...whiteness.

I Don't Do "Make Happy" for Whiteness

"This content isn't appropriate. I'm reporting you."

Listen to them. This is their presumed entitlement to regulate, control, police, and seize upon anything we produce. This is exactly that same core sentiment that killed Ahmaud Arbery and Sean Reed.

Beyond our business persona, work assignments, projects, presentations, and Zoom team meetings, we and our loved ones are the Ahmaud Arbery's, the Sean Reed's, and also the Sandra Bland's.

> **Dr. Susan Jenkins** here, and I'm speaking. I choose my community, family, and self. Facing violence, hate, and ignorance, I make a conscious choice each day to do what is right, be a role model, and contribute. This work keeps me going even though I am afraid much of the time. I am immensely proud to be an African American woman and always will be.

And we are not okay. We are navigating terror and trauma.

While they focus on how to career pivot and work more productively from home, we're consumed by the life and death immediacy of both the 'Rona and being killed by racist cops or self-deputized white supremacists.

We're figuring out how to access a covid19 test, how to be mask-safe in white spaces, how to not get slammed to the pavement for a physical distancing mistake, how to not get shot, how to stay alive.

So pardon me if I give zero fucks for them not liking or appreciating my content. Pardon me if I take a hard pass on learning all the cool features of Zoom meetings.

Not okay.

Anti-Maskers Do Breed, Ya Know

I'm not convinced that ya' can't fix stupid, but I am convinced that willful ignorance in the face of science, facts, evidence is too far gone to be saved. I was never a fan of the *Purge* movie franchise, but one can see the underlying point.

Anti-maskers are the culmination of whiteness gone wild, delusion, and cult all rolled into a no-longer-recognizable human package. Masks are the new IQ tests, and we see which folks are failing. Just sayin.' Here in Houston, it would appear that the denser the population, the *denser* the population, as the saying goes.

Anti-maskers continue to be the main reason why I do NOT enter businesses that don't require masks, and they are the reason I rarely go inside grocery stores or other business establishments that do have a mask requirement they've posted at the entrance. Let me explain.

Whiteness has never had any problem policing Black bodies and Black behavior in public spaces, but whiteness does nothing when it comes to white folks refusing to wear masks because they equate it to an infringement on freedom and compare it to slavery! Hmph. I predict that anti-maskers will soon be "going through some thangs."

Just like Central Park Karen, who felt that posted rules didn't apply to her, anti-maskers ignore signs requiring masks. When I am in the grocery store, I'm counting the individuals without masks and with each one, my anxiety levels are rising with each idiot I spot. Not only do I take issue with the anti-maskers but also with company management that posts a sign that it doesn't even enforce.

I wonder what would happen if the majority of anti-maskers were Black, and the majority of mask wearers were white. Guess we know what the narrative would be.

Here's *my* narrative. Anti-maskers should not be prioritized for care if they contract the virus. Begrudgingly, I'll concede that they should receive some semblance of care but definitely not at the expense of those needing care that abided by the mandates and regulations.

As for me? I always wear a mask in public because that's what decent humans do who live in a society with people who each act in ways that contribute to the greater good of all.

I hate, though, that my mask covers up the majority of my face and hides my "what the fuck is wrong with you?!" expression when I encounter these anti-masker morons. My, husband, however, told me not to worry because "your eyes get the job done."

Whiteness is Bigger in Texas

Lawd, imagine mask-less white folks in Texas protesting during covid—where many people are contracting the virus daily, where people are dying from the virus. Now imagine you could zoom in on the actual protest signs they're carrying and listen in on the words they are loudly chanting – "Bar lives matter" and "Texas bars fight back." It would appear that these folks are fighting for their right to bar hop during a pandemic.

Can I just pause for moment on that whole "bar lives matter" nonsense? Really?!? Privilege at its finest! See. Now that's some white people stuff right there. The sheer and utter caucacity! And then they breed and pass on whiteness to their children. Bless they lil' hearts.

Where is the regard for humanity? Do they not realize that it's not just Black and Brown folks affected by covid? White folks do also get the virus. Plus, the virus is non-partisan and doesn't steer clear of MAGAts the way we do.

This is big news in Texas. Meanwhile, no news on whether a vaccine is underway to treat stupid. Until one is developed, I feel like serving them up a drink myself.

I'm mixing together 3 parts privilege, 2 parts entitlement, and a heavy dose of Black Lives Matter mockery. Then shake—not stir—with a "what about my rights" sentiment gone rogue. Strip away empathy and selflessness.

And what do you get?

Texas.

Where everything is bigger.

Everything.

Bigots.

And especially the covidiots.

History and current circumstances bear out that Texas is the Karen of all the states! Someone recently reminded me that Texas has a history of seceding or threatening to secede. It's what Texas does—it calls the manager. Lawd hammercy. Smh.

Entitled protesters stormed the state capitol to speak to the "manager," upset that the governor mandated bars be shut down in order to help slow the spread of covid. More than 30 bar owners are suing.[21] Their position is that bar closings are a violation of their constitutional rights. I challenge any of them to even spell "constitutional."

Yeah, that's where I am with this dumbfuckery. The mockery, the hypocrisy, the hate, the selfishness, the

---

[21] "More Than 30 Texas Bars Sue Over Gov. Greg Abbott's Recent Shutdown Order." Mitchell Ferman. *Texas Tribune*. 06/29/2020.

entitlement...ugh. What the hell is wrong with white people?!? Don't answer. You know the drill. It's rhetorical. People are dying, and they are upset about bars closing.

And not to be overlooked, isn't it incredible that white folks can protest without the police beatings, the shooting, the arresting, or the gassing? Funny how that works out. In this great demoKKKratic nation, protesting when WE do it has ALWAYS been on the list of threats we face. Another fact to let sink in.

> **Michelle McFarland-McDaniels** here, and I'm speaking. Black lives matter, and we must conduct ourselves, treat each other and compel all others to treat us in a manner that affirms this truth. We must use our individual and collective power to demand justice and create opportunities for ourselves and each other. We don't need any external validation or approval, and we should not wait for any.

U.S. Epicenter for Covid and Racism

It isn't news that we were the only ones NOT surprised that the killing of Black folks during a pandemic wouldn't slow down during a pandemic. When it comes to racism, which is big business, it's business as usual no matter what.

When the ACLU came out with their report that "fatal shootings by police officers did not appear to ease up...and [that] Blacks, Latinos, and Native Americans continue to be disproportionately affected by deadly police shootings compared to white people,"[22] I could feel our collective eye-roll.

ACLU's statement about their hypothesis that killings would slow down was basically "we were wrong."

Will various organizations with the different studies and findings soon be finished with the evidence gathering and pronouncement stages? When can we advance to the "take action" phase?

The 'Rona Exposed Racism as the Big Business It Always Was

Anti-Black racism is sanctioned, endorsed, encouraged, cele-brated, promoted.

It benefits white people, and it sickens and kills us.

Straight up truth.

But white folks want us to stop talking about it, get over it, and move on.

See, alla this right here is what we NOT finna do!

Titanic in Nature

Ever wonder what it must have been like for those poor souls who were aboard the Titanic when it sank in 1912, many of whom lost their lives?

The parallels between the Titanic disaster and the way this pandemic is playing out in the states are mind-blowing.

- Titanic, as a "superpower" ship, was the largest and grandest ship of its time.

---

[22] "Coronavirus Pandemic Didn't Curb Fatal Police Shootings, ACLU Report Finds." Erik Ortiz. nbcnews.com. 08/19/2020.

- Multiple critical warnings or "briefings" were not heeded.
- Titanic barreled ahead "business as usual" at full speed in an ice field despite the known dangers.
- Not enough life-saving "PPE" equipment.
- Conflict of interest between safety and profit.
- Infrastructure deficiencies of the ship.
- Planned lifeboat drill that could have saved many lives cancelled due to a decision by the ship's captain.
- A class/status system that helped determine survivors and victims.
- Great proportionate loss to the frontline crew.
- Third-class passengers disadvantaged due to lack of access to life-saving "PPE" equipment.
- Delay of 30-minutes by ship's captain contributed to loss of life in a catastrophe that took only 2 hours and 40 minutes to play out.
- Many passengers remained in denial that there was anything seriously wrong and were slow to act until it became blatantly obvious that the ship would sink.
- Life-saving measures were ignored and unheeded because people had a hard time believing that a ship as grand as Titanic could sink.
- Devoted "frontline" band musicians knew the ship was sinking and yet "played on" doing their job so as to provide comfort to others.
- First-class passengers were afforded the dignified choice to live or die while the decision to live or die for steerage passengers was made for them.
- The guns of the ship's crew officers ensured proper monopolization of the "collective PPE" lifeboats.

- More lives could've been saved with better real-time strategy and leadership.
- The chairman of the cruise line who snagged a spot on a lifeboat took "no responsibility at all" for the disaster that took the lives of more than 1500 people.

The sinking of the Titanic is one of the most tragic events involving loss of life at sea and also the most preventable. Both the commentary written about the tragedy and the Titanic's legacy have an eery similarity to the gross mismanagement of the pandemic as well as to the denial of some that there even is a pandemic. The mismanagement and denial, coupled with existing racism, have proven deadly to us and other communities of color.

Orange Is the New White

The epicenter for both pandemics is the orange squatter menace that sits in the big house. I have a need to document just that one line and have it be a part of this book's official record. That line by itself is the everyday daily summary and update. It's the main thing we need to know. No need for us to tune in to the news.

Other than all that, everything is "great again." Things were shitty for us before 2016. Things are super shitty after. White supremacy strongly felt that after 8 years, it needed to seize back the presidency and install *this* man to run the country.

Person, woman, man, camera, TV.

I'm so done with this shitshow.

And through the sheer blaxhaustion of it all, I have retained the energy to laugh at how pathetic it is to see white dumbfuckery on display every damn day. So shameful. How embarrassing for them that this is the best whiteness has to offer after 8 years of a zero-scandal Black president.

I will cringe more than ever at the words "your superior" in any context. So hard to not think that just as evil steals, kills, and destroys everything in its wake, so too has whiteness destroyed so much. The terms "supremacy" and "superiority" that whiteness traffics in are mere pseudonyms for mediocrity, evil, and hate. In no language can I aptly express what a mess of things whiteness has made.

And though the supreme orange one represents all that is wrong, he is not solely to blame. Whiteness always needs both white cooperation and white silence from the pack. He has enjoyed both.

Corona Living While Black

Folks are talking about high risk and pre-existing conditions. Well guess what. Being Black is high risk. Being Black is also a pre-existing condition.

The glaring racial disparities laid bare in the coronavirus era provide us with the additional stressors of corona living while Black.

Will I be stopped for looking suspicious and threatening while wearing a face mask?

Am I better off not venturing out at dark while wearing a mask?

Will I be turned away for a test?

Will my symptoms be dismissed?

Will my symptoms be attributed to something else?

Will I be given ventilator privilege and priority?

Will I receive the same quality of healthcare and level of service if I test positive?

Will this be the year that gives them the excuse to try and kill us all?

Corona Working While Black

The new buzz word for work this year is pivot. Each of us was driven to pivot due to the new circumstances we found ourselves in with the lockdown and enforced social distancing.

Depending on the nature of our work, a fair amount of us managed through the pivot. Wanna know what else managed through the pivot? Racism. Yes, racism took a pivot, too, in the form of racist Zoombombing. Committed hate will always find a way.

In response to all the reports of racist Zoombombings, I took to social media in March to ask Zoom CEO Eric Yuan about his plans to tackle this, especially in light of over 100 million Zoom users leveraging the platform for business and school. As we head to print ahead of a December release, nothing but crickets from Mr. Yuan or anyone at Zoom on his behalf.

It should not have come as a surprise to anyone that with racism on the rise, so too would be Zoombombing. And just like all else our covid 2020 vision revealed, what existed before coronavirus now exists alongside coronavirus. The insidious nature of racism finds innovative ways to reinvent and express itself with the help of technology.

> **Tiffany Salmon** here, and I'm speaking. In my experience, working in corporate America while Black has been a game of Russian Roulette. With each offer comes a poison to pick: being paid a touch over the poverty line, no health insurance, no sick days, or no vacation time, all while enduring the surety of microaggressions, lack of promotion, and willful ignorance.

Past and present tell us that our daily lived experiences with racism have never been enough to prompt swift action and condemnation against racial acts. Though, for example, New York City schools banned the use of Zoom in favor of another platform, there's been no concerted initiative or movement—corporate or otherwise—focused on our psychological or emotional safety in virtual spaces.

I'm still waiting to see what happens on this front, especially with the assumption being that we'll be video-zooming instead of audio-conferencing. Racism is still an issue even with a remote workforce. Microaggressions are still an issue with a remote workforce. I'm just not hearing as much from leadership as we should be at this point about a "digital pivot" for anti-racism, equity, and inclusion that aligns with our new normal.

One of the break-out room assignments that I give to leaders in my CARE™ course—Conversations About Racial Experiences™—is to discuss and strategize how they would respond and what measures they would take during a Zoom team meeting if a team member's background prominently displayed an "All Lives Matter" sign. Without going into detail, let's just say that we have every reason to be worried about assaults on our psychological and emotional safety and well-being during vir-tual team meetings. Sigh.

How They Live the Covid Life

The 'Rona continues to systematically reveal who they are and always have been. It's mostly the "good" white folks who in their persistent denial cry out with claims of "this is not who we are." No, boo. This is exactly who y'all are. In addition to what I've already said, I am going down a recent memory lane of gun shops in some states that remained open as part of "essential" business even though the experts confirmed that shooting the virus is not effective.

In California, a state that closed its gun shops, the NRA is suing the state for the closings and for declaring gun shops non-essential. You really can't make up this dumbfuckery.

And in my same trip down recent memory lane, the libraries and bookstores that were closed nationwide did not result in one peep of concern or protest and did not garner any lawsuits.

And the decision to shut down schools and yet leave open bars and restaurants...I can't even. Sigh.

That something is seriously wrong brings me to the issue of entitlement when it marries up with lack of empathy and compassion. Both empathy and compassion contribute greatly to what makes a person human. Just as I learned that relatives aren't necessarily family, I'm also learning that personhood doesn't necessarily confer humanness on the inhabiter of a body.

And you need both traits to fight against both pandemics of covid and racism.

When empathy and compassion go missing, it contributes greatly to the guaranteed perpetuation of both pandemics.

White folks engaged in more advocacy and outrage over statues, bars, and mask-less rights than over the loss of lives—Black or otherwise. Whiteness doesn't even pretend to take the moral high road. Whiteness is both Karen and Jan all at once and at the same time.

Talk about this being the year for centering white dissatisfaction! Angry white people get to congregate and complain about "losing their freedom" while being allowed to show up with shotguns and assault rifles.

What do you think would happen to a crowd of us assembling in public to complain about [insert any reason] while armed with shotguns and assault rifles—or carrying toy guns or cell phones or skittles, for that matter? Yeah, too many hashtags to count. Too many choruses of "say their names."

Can we be sure that white folks didn't take a pledge of allegiance to hypocrisy when they reached a certain age. Did they get a learner's permit or something? Do they have a certified and bona fide membership card? Maybe there's even some type of secret initiation ceremony. I know. Just spit-balling here. Trying to make it make sense.

In other news, a 14-year-old unarmed Black youth, on suspicion—*only the suspicion*—of having marijuana, was just recently tackled, slammed to the ground, and beat down with "justifiable force" by pattyrollers.

> **Shelly-Ann Wilson Henry** here, and I'm speaking. I'm an accomplished black woman. When you label me disgruntled (a.k.a. angry), tell me I don't smile enough or I'm too assertive, and call me a troublemaker because I challenge the status quo, you're telling me to know my place. I wouldn't be here if my ancestors knew their place. NO, I WILL NOT FIT IN TO MAKE YOU COMFORTABLE!

Essentially, No

"I am not going back."

Five words in late July that my sister was repeating at will without wavering.

She is a teacher in Florida, which at several points during this year was one of our country's hotspot states—a state highlighted by the media almost daily due to its surging covid crisis and to the talent of its governor renowned for his impersonations of 45.

Specifically, she teaches in Jacksonville, which also happens to be the city that was scheduled to host the Republican National Convention until political leadership determined that the danger was too high to risk convening there.

You likely remember because it was during this time that the grand talk was that children and teachers must return to school. Why? Because it was important. Can you feel the side-eye I'm dishing up with this paragraph?

There is no convincing me that any of this mandate crap makes sense right now. That this country has lost its way to such the extent that it is willing to risk the lives of children and teachers is beyond shameful and appalling. As we know, there are alternatives to in-person instruction that would save lives and allow our children to continue learning.

Anyway, amidst all of this back-to-school drama, my sister and other teachers were receiving offers of legal assistance with living wills and were being advised to review their life insurance policies. Seriously, you can't make up this dumb-fuckery. I'm no infectious disease expert or pandemic expert, but if it's serious enough to warrant beefing up one's living will and life insurance, then maybe teachers and students should not be going back.

And for teachers, specifically, they were overworked, underpaid, and not respected before covid. But now these same overworked, underpaid, disrespected teachers are ex-pected to be sacrificial lambs.

Plus, my sister and other teachers are discovering that there will be no enforcing of 6ft of distance and that there are no regular and consistent protocols for disinfecting classrooms. Whew boy!

So what did my sister do?

She applied for an exception, also known as permission, to teach exclusively online rather than teach in person. At the time of this writing, she hadn't received THE decision but has made HER decision already.

Unless something drastic changes, five words.

She is not going back.

Covid Lays it Bare

At last count, more than 20 cities and counties have declared racism a public health crisis. Kinda late, don't cha think?

If only they had been listening.

If only so many of us being killed had registered on their radar screens.

If only those workplace discrimination lawsuits had provided a clue, and so on and so on.

On the one hand, I want to shout hallelujah from the rooftops that 20 cities and counties have seen the light and have named it. Another part of me, the exhausted we-told-ya-so part, wants to point out that we had to wait until our experience was confirmed by others before it could be validated as our experience. Ugh. Grrr.

> **Debbie Holmes** here, and I'm speaking. You said you couldn't hear me? Oh, I get it. You can't hear me because you see me. You didn't understand me? It's not my words, but the meaning behind my words you should understand. You don't want me to speak? Beware it's not my spoken words, but my thoughts you should fear. Like I said, I'm speaking damn it!

Anyhoo, as we all know, living Black in this country was ALWAYS a health hazard long before the 'Rona hit. It's a well-being hazard, a breathing hazard!

Non-Essential Essentials (A Poem)

we see what you do
turning the world upside down

where essential is non-essential
and non-essential is essential
where truth is lie
and lie is truth
where news is fake
and fake is news
where science is hoax
and hoax is science
where racism is patriotism
and patriotism is racism
where peace is riot
and riot is peace
where honor is shame
and shame is honor

we see what you do
giving death blows brand-new life

— \o/ tmr

ACT IV

Great White Lies

White supremacy is the source of all great white lies.

Ain't a Damn Thang Fragile About Whiteness

First and foremost, serious question: What the hell do white folks have to be fragile about?!? They own nearly every-damn-thing! They control nearly every-damn-thing! So then, what? Seriously, what?

Nothing.

Not. A. Damn. Thing.

> **Jonee Meiser** here, and I'm speaking. When white people enter a conversation about racism, it is not a conversation for them to dictate, but they will try to control the conversation to prioritize their comfort. Racism will continue to thrive if white people don't confront their feelings. Their hurt feelings do NOT equate to countless black lives lost. The threats to our lives are a direct result of their inability to face and unpack their biases.

But yet and still, white folks clamor over and embrace fragility like it's the golden ticket that exonerates them from owning up to racism.

The fragility narrative explains away their discomfort about race with platitudes designed to avoid casting whiteness as evil and to avoid casting those that worship and uphold it as immoral and inhumane monsters.

The creator and purveyor of the fragility brand—no surprise—is a white woman who is making bank because she figured out a way to cash in on gullible white folks who would rather justify away their racism rather than confront their whiteness preservation system™ (WPS), which when triggered acts out like this—

- crying (exhibited by white women)
- screaming and yelling (mostly exhibited by white men, but white women have shown that they can go shrill)
- insisting "I don't see color" or referencing "Some of my closest friends are Black"
- tone-policing
- gaslighting attacks
- avoiding the topic of race altogether
- accusing us of "reverse racism" (as if there were such a thing, and as if only the non-reverse racism is okay)

Think about it. The idea of "white fragility" is extremely problematic in perpetuating the myth that white people are entitled to be comfortable. She may not have sold as many books, but I'm thinking this title along with content that has more substance and accountability would be more appropriate—"*Avoidance and Defensive Tactics that White People Employ to Maintain Privilege and White Supremacy While Perpetuating Racism.*" You're welcome, Robin DiAngelo.

Anyhoo, per the usual…Black women have been sounding the alarm about buying into that "white fragility" nonsense. We have been on the receiving end of too much hate, rage, and killing to equate any of that to some fragility bull. Special shout-out to Karen. All of this fragility stuff plays right into her wheelhouse.

Fragility was extremely problematic from the very beginning. It gets white folks off the hook with a gentle way to characterize and minimize their rage, defensiveness, visceral discomfort, indignation, jealousy, entitlement, etc.—all of which emanate from a deeply ingrained WHITENESS PRESERVATION SYSTEM™ (WPS) integral to the perpetuation of white supremacy that keeps us oppressed and disenfranchised while keeping whiteness elevated and prioritized.

White fragility supports the popular "I am a good person" false narrative.

White fragility strengthens the trope of delicate whiteness.

White fragility wrongly confers an "It's a natural reaction" victim status on whiteness.

Guuurrrllll, this misguided term has single-handedly done more harm than good. Meanwhile, our voices continue to be decentered from conversations that focus on race and racism by white folks flocking to pay a white woman to learn about their fragility and help them justify it.

What they feel is NOT fragility.

> **Keyonna A. Monroe** here, and I'm speaking. I am not your competition. I am not here as your exotic sexual fetish, nor do I exist to serve only as your backbone and strength in areas of your weakness. I am to be heard, respected, and valued in all gloriousness as a woman who's earned the right to take up space and make an impact.

And if white folks did the work deep down, then they, like us, would know exactly what it is they're feeling. Hmph. Fragility, my ass! Gimme a break!

For any of my sisters who are supporters of the book of the same name, slow yo' roll. I'm not suggesting that the book itself has not resulted in some good in the sense that some white folks recognized it for what it was and determined to go deeper on their own beyond the inadequate fragility paradigm.

The danger is that fragility for many has become a one-stop shop and a justification to continue with soft unconscious bias training and tread carefully on anti-Black racism education. Learnings based on unconscious bias and other fragility frameworks benefit whiteness. Centers whiteness. At the expense of us. The whole body of deflection and deception—which fragility is a part of—is white supremacy psychology genius. And it contributes to a lack of substantial gains in dismantling anti-Black racism.

Both the paradigm and the semantics of fragility are very problematic. That's why I refer to a whiteness preservation system™ (WPS) that embodies a direct responsibility and ownership in keeping us and non-Black POC down and "othered." Framing the conversation around fragility does nothing to fundamentally shift things. While they are focused on their hurt feelings, more Black bodies are being killed. Ain't nobody but white folks like Robin DiAngelo and her trainer disciples got the time or luxury to walk other white folks through their feelings at such a high and deadly price to US.

Further think about it this way – fragility is the repackaging of white supremacy with justification of one's WPS such that white supremacy can be protected. The strategy has always been to pivot to a more palatable alternative rather than to call a thing a thing. Fragility works better for white folks' conscience. That they remain comfortable with the lie of their superiority is paramount to continuation of whiteness.

I am against any teaching that gets white folks off the hook or makes it easy for them to minimize their role in perpetuating a system of white supremacy and racism. They play a huge part—either inadvertently or more directly—in this system. Black women are constantly on the receiving end of racism and misogynoir, and we rarely receive consideration of prioritization of our feelings. White feelings, however, are enough to threaten and kill Black lives and careers. So, let me put things in perspective for us. When it comes to white feelings, there's a *Gone with the Wind* reference they will understand. It perfectly captures our prevailing sentiment. "Frankly, my dears, we don't give a damn."

See How Whiteness Works

Let's call a thing a thing.
White supremacy.
White supremacy.
White supremacy.
Also let it sink in that Black Lives Matter and objections to racism are being called a "cultural divide." This euphemistic privilege deflects from and minimizes what has always been THE issue in this country—white supremacy. No amount of feigned ignorance, fragility, or wordsmithing can hide the reality. White supremacy—with all of its hateful manifestations—is the mother threat that has spawned all other threats. There's no white sugar-coating that makes it less than what it is. White supremacy is baked into institutions because it is THE foundation for everything. The foundation makes systemic racism possible.

White supremacy and its sibling racism are the sources of the greatest injustices ever perpetuated in this country. These two siblings explain why Black Lives Matter—the reality and the movement—garners so much visceral resistance and vehement push-back. Black Lives Matter is not a cause or political statement. It is an affirmation of the reality of our humanity.

Is it not the case that white folks have politicized our lives and turned it into a debate, much the same way they have politicized the wearing of masks?

Was it not white folks who turned their "right" to own humans into a war?

White folks' indoctrination into whiteness detached them from their humanity. So yeah, historically, white folks are accustomed to trading Black humanity for white inhumanity. That's right. Consider that whiteness handcuffed a shot and paralyzed Jacob Blake to his hospital bed and granted patriot status to a white male assault-rifle-wielding killer.

To acknowledge that Black lives matter is to acknowledge and thus expose white supremacy as a lie. A BIG PHAT BOLD-FACED WHITE LIE.

And the lie of white supremacy has given birth to a slew of lies, one of which is that anything other than whiteness is less than.

And they eat up and devour the lie like the pitiful self-worth-starved souls they are. All the while fetishizing and lusting after Black bodies. All the while stealing intellectual property, appropriating our culture, and exploiting our labor. All the while tanning to get darker, getting lip injections to get fuller lips, and getting butt implants to get thicker. I mean, next level fucked-up shit that by itself turns white supremacy on its head.

Even in instances of non-literal or non-impending life and death, whiteness manages to rage. Take, for examples, the renewed celebration of *Black Panther* upon the passing of Chadwick Boseman and the celebration of Blackness by Beyonce in her *Black is King* video. There are so many examples, both past and present, but these two were standouts of 2020 due to the iconic status of the former and the Disney association of the latter. In each case, the centering and celebrating of Blackness threatened the status quo of white supremacy.

That's it.

It's that simple.

It's that predictable.

We know why there is ALWAYS a "blacklash" against

Black Lives Matter

Black Power

Black Panthers

Black is Beautiful

Black Empowerment

Superiority is not superiority unless there is "inferiority." For the system of white supremacy to be maintained, it must depend ENTIRELY upon Black oppression and anti-Black racism across all systems, across all industries, and across all hearts and minds.

The driving force of white supremacy and whiteness can be captured in two main questions:

1. How can we maintain power?
2. How can we maintain dominance?

Both questions and their answers remain primary threats to us.

> **Etta Jacques Jones** here, and I'm speaking. I believe in my bones that we inherited strength, perseverance, and intelligence from our ancestors. We've exercised muscles others have had the lifelong privilege of allowing to atrophy. And that makes us better. Yes, better. But don't take advantage. We are NOT magic. We feel emotional and physical pain. We bleed and we get tired. Fuck magic.
> We worked harder.

Sounds About White

We know. We always know. We are not deceived by the "poli-tricks," the constant gaslighting, and the "methinks they doth protesteth too much." White folks do a whole lot of projecting and deflecting.

> **Teeona Mayberry** here, and I'm speaking. You act like you want change and then allow mediocrity to prevail. What good is your voice if action never follows? I refuse to be muted in rooms where decisions are made. You cannot dim what was meant to shine bright; you can't and won't ever dim ME. Sorry! Your privilege is no longer the desired currency in this place. Excuse me while I go prosper, effortlessly!

"Diversity educator" Jane Elliott's question to white folks about which of them would trade places with us is quite telling. White folks and non-Black POC know that to be Black is to be the most hated in our society. So none of them would willingly trade places with us.

The "power of normal" that whiteness bestows is just too good and convenient to give up. Whiteness, after all, is the default for how people are grouped in the system. Whiteness doesn't get the hyphen like African-Americans do (or like Asian-Americans, Mexican-Americans, etc.). Why? To be white is to be American. America is "the land of the free and the home of the brave" aka whiteness.

Whiteness also doesn't have its hair care products relegated to the "ethnic hair care products" section of the store aisle. I even have a personal rule related to this. I vowed when

I was a graduate student at Cornell that I would never again take up residence in a city where I can't easily find Black hair care products or a Black hair salon. For obvious reasons, a city like that would not be the place for me no way.

> **Dee Perry** here, and I'm Speaking. I'm exhausted. NO, I'M EXASPERATED! As I sit in another "inclusion activity," the prompt states, "What did you do over the weekend?" Sigh. They will never understand the historical ritual passed down by my ancestors called "wash day" and the two-day process of maintaining my beautifully curly 4c locs. So instead, I share a socially white construct to limit confusion, blank stares and additional microaggressions... I baked cookies.

So, if identity, public spaces, goods and services cater to whiteness and segregate us and our needs into "special" sections, then how far have we really come since Jim Crow? Not much. They removed the "whites only" and "coloreds only" signs but left the mindset and the practices intact. Hmph. Hunty, I'ma 'bout ta tell ya somethin.' They still Jim Crowin' us. Just like they still pattyrollin' us.

They ain't about to trade status and position with us. They too busy enjoying their whiteness and moving in the world with an expectation that their needs be readily met and with an entitlement that demands it. We move through the world knowing that we and our needs are in the margins—at best.

Think about a child who is spoiled due to getting everything they want and screaming until they do. Think about a child being so indulged and never accepting the word "no."

Now think about the ass-whoopin' this child needs and never got.

For more than 400 years, the combined three forces of white supremacy, white privilege, and anti-Black racism have provided lavishly for white folks. Decentering whiteness and achieving racial equity and social justice is terrifying for them. They feel threatened by the thought of losing dominance and becoming minoritized. They will fight like hell to not be in that position and to maintain their power. What we're witnessing with the de-evolution of the Republican party under Trumpism is a good example of how this plays out. Power will do anything – and I mean anything—to hold on to power.

I have no doubt in my mind that cis hetero non-disabled white men that are committed to white supremacy would not hesitate to re-enslave us if they knew they could get away with it. Doubt it? Consider from a few months ago Senator Tim Cotton's description of slavery as a "necessary evil." (The fact that his last name is Cotton is just a scary coincidence.) Subjugation and oppression are part and parcel of white supremacy 101. Like many others, he knows exactly what he says and the implications. Whiteness has to operate in ways that fundamentally keep things unequal between Black and white.

If we understand this, we won't continue to waste our energy questioning why it is taking so long for this such-and-such to happen or for that such-and-such to happen. There is NO unified plan for white folks to dismantle white supremacy or end anti-Black racism. None.

If there were, it would have been achieved already. They are the only ones who can dismantle both, so if it ain't happened by now, it's cuz they don't want it to happen. Period. The white power elite likes things just the way they are. Whiteness is generationally ingrained, historically ingrained, traditionally ingrained, politically ingrained, socially ingrained, educationally ingrained, etc.

Hell, it's encoded.

Them on top. Us on the bottom.

Sound about white?

White Mediocrity

If whiteness were as superior as all the white-washing of everything makes it appear to be, then why would whiteness feel threatened by, fearful of, and enraged by Blackness or otherness that shows up with excellence, beauty, leadership, light, and truth?

It's not an actual question, y'all. Part of the blaxhaustion is trying to wrap my head around the sheer ignorance and hate of it all. Nothing can make this make sense.

So-called white superiority confident in its superiority does not operate in the way we've been experiencing it. The only thing that feels, thinks, talks, and acts like that is nothing but straight-up mediocre whiteness at best.

> **Sedruola Maruska** here, and I'm speaking. I looked within and cowered at my own brilliance. That's when I understood you fear me to the point of wanting to destroy me. Because If you never allow me to shine, I cannot illuminate the ugliness you've inflicted. I'm unleashed. Come celebrate my luminosity, or step aside while I shine.

And mediocre whiteness elevates itself by projecting inferiority onto Blackness. Whiteness as a social construct masquerades itself as power, an ethnicity, and a personal identity.

168

That's all it's ever been—social supremacy translated into a skin tone. That's not the same thing as a culture, or even a people.

They don't even know who they really are, which makes them susceptible and gullible to the lie.

Blue-Collar and Blue-Uniform Rage

They're both different "species" of the same beast. And they both thrive on white-collar silence. The hoods never came off. They got replaced by police uniforms, corporate suit and tie, high heels, and also justice robes.

Check this out. Fair Wayne Bryant, a Black man, got life for stealing hedge clippers, and the Louisiana Supreme Court ruled nearly unanimously that it's fair! If that don't scream "systemic racism" to all the denying white folks then I don't know what does. It's clear as black and white. Just another in a long list of shameful examples.

Specifically, Mr. Bryant's sentencing fate is the modern-day version of "Pig Laws" which were instituted during Reconstruction with the aim of enslaving newly freed Blacks into poverty. Slavery 2.0.

Chief Justice Bernette Johnson, "the lone Black judge on the bench was the only one out of seven to disagree." She is also "the court's first Black Chief Justice."

In her scathing dissent, she emphasized that "Mr. Bryant has already spent nearly 23 years in prison and is now over 60 years old. If he lives another 20 years, Louisiana taxpayers will have paid almost one million dollars to punish Mr. Bryant for his failed effort to steal a set of hedge clippers. This man's life sentence for a failed attempt to steal a set of hedge clippers is grossly out of proportion to the crime and serves no legitimate penal purpose.[23]

"No legitimate penal purpose." Hmm. That's where I disagree with SistahQueen Justice Johnson. It does serve a purpose. It reinforces the power of whiteness to legislate our oppression and it upholds systemic racism as legally sanctioned.

Roger Stone was found guilty on 7 different charges and is walking around free. Aunt Becky was found guilty on university admission fraud charges and got sentenced to white woman camp-style jail for two months and will likely be out to spend Christmas with her co-conspirator family members. Isn't justice grand?

Stoked by and vulnerable to the rhetoric of hate and fear and the nostalgia of their greatness, white lies are their lifeblood.

Driven by and drunk with power and profit while hiding behind their performative show of wokeness, white-collar racists capitalize on living both side-ism.

Again, the common thread is a pathologically ingrained belief in the superiority of whiteness which was created by white skin to grant whiteness entitlement to do pretty much whatever they hell they want when it comes to us. Are we the only ones to see just how sick and twisted is whiteness? Historically, presently, and repeatedly, acts of violence and horror have been perpetuated by whiteness because, yeah, superiority. Superiority, y'all! I ain't seein' it.

---

[23] "He Got Life for Stealing Hedge Clippers. The Louisiana Supreme Court Says it's a Fair Sentence." Teo Armus. *The Washington Post*. 08/05/2020.

Shirley Ebikebina Moser-Onduru here, and I'm speaking. Black: "Dismal, gloomy, or forbidding, like darkness; destitute of moral light or goodness; atrociously wicked; cruel; mournful; calamitous; horrible" (Webster's 1913 Dictionary). Sadly, this is people's perception of individuals from African origins and their lived experiences. It is time to change this description. It is an offence to be called Black! Call me Brown-Skin/Person-of-Colour/Nigerian/African because this is who I am.

Qualified Immunity = Killing Impunity

Hmph. Qualified immunity. A sham doctrine like this one is yet another example of how racism gets "baked" into laws, policies, institutions, etc.

Qualified immunity, a judiciary invented legal defense, shields police from liability and protects them from having to face any consequences from wrongdoing. Hmph. It's basically a free pass for the po-po to terrorize and kill us. That's how I read it, and it appears that's how the po-po are reading it, too, if history is any indication.

For example, Derek Chauvin, who killed George Floyd will likely be playing the qualified immunity card in a civil suit.

With qualified immunity in play for police and "stand your ground" in play for civilians, along with how both are appLIEd and (ab)used, this tells us everything we need to know about the designated recipients and beneficiaries of law and order.

Ironically, the Constitution itself emboldens whiteness to dehumanize Blackness to uphold whiteness. And every time I think about the hand they place on the Bible to swear an oath, I envision their entire hand itself bursting into flames. It is a mockery of the oath and a mockery of the Bible.

Final word on qualified immunity?

Threat.

There goes another square on our Black bingo card.

Being on LinkedIn's Most Wanted (to Shut Up) List

White supremacy likes to be bold in how it announces and justifies itself. Having content deleted by the "law-and-order patrols" of LinkedIn is not a first silencing rodeo for me.

LinkedIn likes to trot out that vague language of how I'm "violating professional community policies."

Based on my experiences with the unseen powers of LinkedIn behind the curtain, the reason why certain content is a violation is because of its "audacity" to center a lived experience of Black folks, make white people uncomfortable, remind white people of their racism, implicate the current squatter in the big house, and anger the squatter's supporters.

Common thread here is white feelings.

Threat to us?

Hell yeah!

Star-Bangled Banner (National Anthem of USA)

Serious question. Did we get punked?

Oh, say can you see by the dawn's early light

What so proudly we hailed at the twilight's last gleaming?

Whose broad stripes and bright stars through the perilous fight,

O'er the ramparts we watched were so gallantly streaming.

172

And the rocket's red glare, the bombs bursting in air,

Gave proof through the night that our flag was still there.

Oh, say does that star-spangled banner yet wave

O'er **the land of the free and the home of the brave**
[emphasis mine]?

—Francis Scott Key

> **Dr. Tammy L. Hodo** here, and I'm speaking. As a biracial woman, and military veteran, I refuse to justify my existence. I know my voice does not have as much of an impact in America as white women but I will not be silenced; I will not live in fear, and I will not have another woman tell me where my place is in our society.

Colonizing Murderer Day

One of the many assaults on truth and facts involves that infamous day celebrated in October. I remember when I was a kid in school, we were brainwashed into reciting some lame poem about "in 1492 Columbus sailed the ocean blue."

Here we are in the year 2020, and we're still submitting petitions to flip the switch on this nonsense.

That whiteness remains opposed to recognizing and honoring Indigenous Peoples' Day reveals so much about whiteness and the ones who hold on to it at any cost. It's the mass psychosis and dysfunction of whiteness to convince itself to honor a dead white dude for never stepping foot on U. S soil—a white dude, who along with other white dudes, murdered, raped, infected, and enslaved indigenous peoples and African Americans; and is the source of countless kids and grown-ass people, who should now know better, being conditioned and programmed to believe that this white guy "discovered" America. Hmph.

That Columbus Guy Is AmeriKKKa's Thug Zero

To shift "his-story" to truth and facts while honoring and paying tribute to the rightful owners of the land now called the United States is too inconvenient for whiteness. It goes against "legacy" and "heritage." Whiteness would rather preserve one of the biggest lies of all.

Hell, the guy even got a national holiday despite the historical evidence of who and what he was.

But hey, the guy was white...so there's that.

The guy never stepped foot on U.S. soil. He landed in the Bahamas. Subsequently, he raped, enslaved, infected, and murdered Native Caribbeans, leaving the Native Indian population nearly extinct. He introduced European exploration and a culture of slavery and genocide that has killed countless Native Americans as well as African American slaves.[24]

As sistahQueen Angela Davis puts it, "Black and Native lives are systematically choked by an enduring white supremacy that thrives on oppression and settler colonialism, and is backed by drones, the dispossession of territory and identity to millions, mass incarceration, the un-peopleing of people, and resource grabs."

So just to sum up and be crystal clear, the evil murdering and raping guy is celebrated on Colonizing Murderer Day, a national holiday that has led generations of U.S. Americans to

---

[24] change.org

falsely believe this guy "discovered" America. See how whiteness works.

The same twisted psychology of whiteness worshippers who embrace "his-story" is the same twisted psychology exhibited by Senator Tom Cotton, who referred to the enslavement of African peoples as "the necessary evil upon which the union was built."[25] Nothing can make this make sense except an enduring oppressor mindset that believes that the oppressed deserve their oppression. Cue my eye-roll. This is epic-level whiteness.

This reminds me of the times when my family and I are watching a movie, and something happens in the action that makes absolutely no sense and flies in the face of any explanation. In these moments, my son will matter-of-factly say, "Plot device." In other words, what we just witnessed or heard makes absolutely no sense. The writers and director have the "poetic license" to dictate any and all aspects of the plot to serve any purpose – believable or not. In order for viewers to buy into the plot, they have to suspend belief.

It's no different in real life. Whiteness has the power to dictate the narrative, control the narrative, and even change the narrative mid-stream. Whatever best suits whiteness and whiteness worshippers. Buying into it means not only suspending belief, but also suspending reason, logic, truth, facts, science, one's humanity, etc. You get the idea, right?

For this reason and more, I'm at the point where my default utterance to the shit that white people pull and "believe" is an exasperated "white people!" Insert another eye-roll here.

That there has not been, for example, an embrace of the "1619 Project" or a complete denouncement of a holiday for

---

[25] *"Was Slavery a 'Necessary Evil'? Here's What John Stuart Mill Would Say."* David Lay Williams. The Washington Post. 07/30/2020

"that guy," tells us exactly what frames the narrative and what is being framed.

In the words of James Baldwin, "There are days in this country when you wonder what your role in this country is and your place in it. How precisely are you going to reconcile yourself to your situation here and how you are going to communicate to the vast, heedless, unthinking, cruel white majority that you are here? I am terrified at the moral apathy, the death of the heart, which is happening in my country. These people deluded themselves for so long that they really don't think I'm human. I base this on their conduct, not on what they say. This means that they have become moral monsters."

Check the box again on "threat."

We Are Not Your Stereotypes

I am right now channeling James Baldwin and his "I Am Not Your Negro."

With access to information being at an all-time high with the advent of the Internet, it never ceases to amaze me that ignorance in 2020 is also at an all-time high. I'm talking next-level "ignant."

They got the wrong one. I'm not the happy and contented stereotype whose words and demeanor should smile and dance for the comfort and entertainment of whiteness. I'm a disruptive inclusionist ready with inconvenient and uncomfortable truths. If they didn't know, now they know.

White folks like to get their information about us from a white controlled media that pushes and promotes stereotypical narratives. Whiteness subscribes to a "from whiteness, by whiteness, about them" model that decenters and caricaturizes us.

I'ma take every opportunity I can to bust stereotypes by highlighting our talents, our gifts, our skills, our history, and our experiences.

Why?

Racial stereotypes hurt and harm, compounding our blaxhaustion every time we come up against them.

> **Taye Johnson** here, and I'm speaking. I am the multifaceted black woman that can dispel any stereotype that shadows me. I represent your greatest fear and biggest regret. I stand firm in my truth with an unwavering presence. My self-worth is not based on the approval of the majority. Black women will no longer dim our light in order to help you shine.

The Wall

They already built a wall! A wall of hate. What they need anotha' one fuh? Dumbasses! That is all.

The Original Haters

Our ancestors who were brought to this country and enslaved had to be shaped into a sub-human, non-competitive, defenseless, non-threatening, controllable, pliable class.

This shaping created the optimal condition under which to steal our labor and reveals more about the hate and evil of the *shapers* than it does about the *shapees* whose humanity was denied.

Subtle and blatant forms of this shaping still persist today.

And that tells us everything we need to know about the original and current purveyors of crimes against humanity in this country, crimes against our lives and livelihoods that manifest in our communities, in our workplaces, and even in our homes.

> **Sophia J. Casey** here, and I'm speaking. I'm the embodiment of the answers to the pleading prayers of my ancestors. Although our boldness is consistently attempted to be used as a sword of degradation, we've time and time again grabbed it, made it louder, and used as it as a pillar of fierce vulnerability.

The Upside Down

Truth tellers and justice fighters are ostracized and punished while dissemblers and deniers are lauded and rewarded.

Confidence in one's own ignorance is the new competent.

Obedience, rather than justice, is blind.

Acknowledging or talking about racism is more offensive than racism itself.

Reverse racism implies that there is a right and normal way to do racism.

Unity and Strength Are a Danger to Whiteness

The beneficiaries of whiteness have the most to lose when we come together and unite.

The beneficiaries of whiteness have the most to lose when equality, equity, and justice for all are achieved?

The beneficiaries of whiteness have the most to gain when division and discord are sown?

The beneficiaries of whiteness have the most to gain when inequality, inequity, and injustice are perpetuated?

Whatever we say or do that poses a danger to whiteness, by extension is a threat to us.

Yes, I know it's twisted. Tell me though, what's not twisted about whiteness?

> **Huldah Akita** here, and I'm speaking. Strength is Her; Beauty is Her; Intelligence is Her… I am Her! You may think you have had the power to stop the eruption of my purpose when you set your eyes on my exquisite brown skin. But you cannot stop the Powerful, Intelligent Black Woman. It's Her Time , My time, Our Time!

The Real Thugs and Looters Ain't Us

"We live in a society of an imposed forgetfulness, a society that depends on public amnesia."—Angela Davis

Plenty of historical receipts. Noteworthy is the period in 1919 known as the "Red Summer of Hate." Armed white folks rioted—YES, WHITE FOLKS HAVE A DOCUMENTED PENCHANT FOR RIOTING—in 25 cities. Every instance of hate-filled rioting in these 25 cities was started by whites. They burned, they looted, and they killed thousands of us.

And actually prior to the 1960s, white folks initiated nearly 100% of all race riots in this country. And they are likely the only racial group surprised by this. Cuz I know we sho ain't. They've been reeking havoc in this country since they stepped foot on and raped the land and its people.

But they criticize us for protests. And this year there have been way too many.

Manuel Lewis, another Black man who "died in police custody" March 3 in Tacoma, Washington, after crying out "I can't breathe," is another one of us murdered. His death was finally ruled a homicide and has prompted protests. Justifiably so.

Like George Floyd's May 25 murder, Manuel Ellis died while in handcuffs, and he was restrained by four officers. The official autopsy report is that he was deprived of oxygen—or in other words, he couldn't breathe! Kinda like the big clue he was giving the cops when he kept repeating, "I can't breathe. I can't breathe." Ugh.

News of his murder didn't surface publicly until early June, over a week after George Floyd was killed. The timing of when we learn of these killings coupled with the scores more we don't know about is extremely troubling. The numbers data on Black killings have historically been lower than what is believed to actually be the case for obvious reasons—Black lives are not valued, and Black bodies go missing and are never accounted for.

In response to protests, some white folks though have sought to invalidate *all* protesters based on the actions of *some* looters. In their misguided racist concern over buildings and property, they erase our lives as meaningless in comparison. As Assata Shakur puts it, they "...have always considered their property more important than our lives." These same folks didn't seek to invalidate all police officers based on the murderous actions of some cops against us. But they cried out to invalidate all protests based on the actions of a few bad actors. Again, the hypocrisy of caucacity is a feature not a flaw.

Funny not funny how that works.

> **Rachel Rudo Munyaradzi** here, and I'm speaking. Yes, I speak well and eloquently...but do NOT get it twisted, thinking you've complimented me when you compare Black people and say that I am better! When you shoot and kill our Black sons, you do not check their speech and elocution first! Rather their melanin speaks for them. So know this ... Blacknificent and united we stand!

My Black is Beautiful

"My Black is beautiful."

These four words.

These four words of an 11-year-old Black girl Nevaeh Thomas affirming her value were her response to the racial slurs directed at her. These words were also the reason a 12-year-old white boy brutally beat her.

And so get this! This! "One of the chief things that the court wants to do is get an evaluation to determine what are the underlying factors that are causing this behavior. One of the things that we have seen through this whole shutdown and covid19 is kids have been acting out. Luckily, most of the behavior is pretty minor behavior."[26]

Seriously, you can't make this stuff up! The lengths people will go to in denying anti-Black racism while ascribing it to

---

[26] "'My Black is Beautiful': 11-Year-Old Black Beaten I What Family Said Was a Racially Motivated Attack." Zack Linly. *The Root*. 09/02/20.

something else—like a mental health issue—is mind-boggling! So basically, instead of acknowledging that this kid needs an intensive intervention on how to be a decent human being and NOT be fucking racist, he receives instead the babying treatment from the "fragility" playbook and is awarded with an evaluation to determine the cause of his behavior!!

I can save the court time and identify exactly the underlying factor and the over-riding factor in diagnosing this kkkid.

He is a fucking little racist!

He is likely being groomed to be a "patriot" by his parents or by hate groups that have infiltrated social media.

Or by the big house squatter impersonating a president and his Twitter feed.

That latter possibility is not one that any of us would have been considering before 2016.

What is it called when a country's youngest white citizens are carrying out violence against Black bodies?

And what is it called when a country doesn't hold them or itself accountable?

I call it a white supremacist racist country!

It's official.

Headliner: An Ode to Cathryn (A Poem)

You're royal and regal
The way you glide into the room on oxygen of Queens
passed too soon

All the people and your subjects swoon

You are Queen Mother
There will never ever be another
Mother to your children
Mother to your grandchildren
Mother to your great grandchildren
Mother to your great great grandchildren
And their children's children's children's children

Headliner, the ultimate that's who you are

You waltz onto the scene your every step giving us life
Giving us so much pep

The way you breathe
The way you speak

The way you hold a glass to your lips it's all a treat...to
Queens in Training, ladies in waiting

And just to think...whenever your mouth parts and speaks
The entire arena is at pause
Leaving some to applaud
And other girls clutching their pearls

One thing remains clear, it's your world

And we are held captive by the essence of you

You are the ultimate Headliner
There's no one finer

We are inspired by you

Intrigued by you

In awe of you

We are catapulted into infinity and beyond by you

We are micro 1/16th versions of you picking up and kicking
up wind of you

We are inscribed with the DNA of you

You spoke into us and we speak into each other

For
Headliner, Ode to Cathryn

We
Are
You

—Teddi Williams

> **Cassandra Binkley** here, and I'm speaking. You don't know me, so don't make assumptions. Don't be confused by my calm personality and steady demeanor. You have no idea of the depth of my heart, vision for what's right, and the ends I will go to such to see my children walk freely into their destinies. The fire within me stays lit. Take note.

Kenosha KKKyle, the Patriot

One of the deadliest verses of their religion is Exterminateus 8:46.

Their hypocrisy in all thing is by design.

Defenders and believers preach a sermon to minimize the systemic threat of only a few bad apples, while at the same time they worship a white "patriot" who shoots and kills peace the same way they assault and kill truth.

And they conveniently forget that a few bad apples always spoil the bunch.

When the ballot box came around, more than 67% of white folks cast their votes in secret for white supremacy. And when the public collection plate came around, whiteness openly chipped in $2M in cash money to grant bail to a killer of peace so he could redeem his "get out of racism free" card.

Sistahs, turn to your neighbor, shake your head, and say, "These white folks done lost they evvah lovin' minds!!" A-men!

Drunk on Ignorance and Fear

They're plastered. Lit.
From the ongoing
backwards free-fall
stemming from an embrace and activation of a social experiment known as racial categorizing.

Alas, as was demonstrated by Frankenstein's monster, these experiments never seem to end well for their creators. My admittedly over-simplified version of the story goes like this: Genius Frankenstein succeeded in giving life to the hideous. When the hideous was not widely accepted by ALL members of society, the hideous took revenge against its creator.

Even literature penned by whiteness is chock full of red flags.

This experiment in hideous whiteness is a real-time epic fail.

The signs are everywhere.

The System Ain't Broken

The system is working exactly how it was always designed to work. The founding colonizers and perpetrators of genocide and enslavement of African peoples created a system that would keep whiteness powerful and wealthy while legally guaranteeing the disenfranchisement of others.

That the system somehow became broken is another one of the biggest lies ever brokered. The system has never been broken. It was just never right in the first place.

If we continue to focus on fixing what's not broken, we'll always be spinning our wheels and frustrated.

Inspecting where the band-aids should go.

Evaluating where the screws need to be applied.

Assessing where the patch job needs to be.

We can't fix what's NOT BROKEN and built by white power. We have to deprive it of its lifeblood—our money and our labor.

Burn That Bitch to the Ground

It's NOT about seats at the table. The seats are a distraction. Don't fall for it. It's what they want us to keep doing—
begging for
pleading for
jumping thru hoops for
and eyeing the seats.

Focus. FOCUS. It's the TABLE, HIS TABLE, and the FOUR. LEGS. HOLDING. IT. UP.

The table is the problem. Having a seat at the table is not part of my mission. It's still HIS table and I'm expected to beg, plead, grovel, and convince HIM that I deserve to be there. Everyday! Hayell naw!! I'll take a hard pass.

Power rarely, if ever, concedes its power but engages in measures to retain it.

So, I say that we burn down the table and start over. That's right. We need to burn that bitch down! And then build the right way this time. Sound radical? I hope so. Cuz I'm in agreement with sistahQueen Angela Davis. "Radical simply means 'grasping things at the root.'"

Until such time that we organize and torch it, I'ma continue to build my own tables. Striving for and vying for collapsible folding seats at a table where we're the ones getting served up racist treatment is another threat to add to the list.

> **Simone Wright** here, and I'm speaking. "Oh?
> You're Simone Wright???" "Don't expect to find a job
> with your hair looking like that!" As a Black woman,
> from Canada, who dons her natural hair, I've been
> subjected to certain stereotypes based off the way I
> speak and look. I'm demanding for the moment when
> someone meets me for the first time says, "Oh! Hello
> Simone Wright!"

Payback Porn

Yeah, I know. It doesn't solve anything, but it helps sometimes to keep my anger in check and make me laugh. I started a fantasy life when I became a mother for the first time. When things got too overwhelming with our high-maintenance baby (which was often), I would imagine getting in my car alone and just driving and driving as far away as I could with no destination and no plans. Just to get away from the pressure and the stress. Don't judge me, sisters. My escape porn and the accompanying feelings of freedom from it all were a big help to me during some rough times.

Anyway, I do the same thing when it comes to turning the tables on white folks. My payback porn is typically comical on the surface with serious undertones. Gurl, lemme share some of this good ole' payback porn with you.

Imagine white Bob being stopped, cuffed, slammed to the ground, and told that he "fits the profile." And then when he asks, you respond, "There were reports of a suspicious white man in the area."

Imagine white Patty telling you she's from Maine, and you pressing her with the question, "No, I mean where are you *really* from?" Without missing a beat, hear yourself pressing her with, "I mean where are *your people* from?"

Imagine white Chad is the "only one" in a meeting full of us in which he expresses his view on a topic. After the meeting, see yourself approaching Chad and telling him that everybody in the meeting felt very uncomfortable because he was so aggressive. Also tell him that maybe next time he can have a more agreeable tone.

Imagine being at a company event in which everyone is sharing about their alma mater, and when it's white Cindy's turn as the only white person in the room, she discloses that she attended a non-HBCU. Now hear yourself tell her that you heard that those white colleges are not real colleges and are only for white people who couldn't get into an HBCU. Watch as all the other Black folks in the room nod in agreement.

Imagine you are organizing a conference event on white people in STEM and need to hire workshop leaders. See yourself going out of your way to contract with mostly Black folks with a few token white folks thrown in for good measure.

Imagine calling 911 on Karen because she's one item over the limit in the grammatically incorrect "10 items or less" line. Hear yourself in a panicky voice lying to the 911 operator that Karen is threatening to hit you with a can of corn, and you're in fear for your life so send the cops right away. Now see the cops arriving, cuffing her, and hauling her ass off to jail.

Ahh. Payback porn.

The Sheer and Utter Caucacity!

The nerve! Boldness coupled with entitlement. Whiteness is so full of itself. Whiteness inserts itself everywhere. That is all.

Come Celebrate with Me (A Poem)

won't you celebrate with me
what i have shaped into
a kind of life? i had no model.
born in babylon
both nonwhite and woman
what did i see to be except myself?
i made it up
here on this bridge between
starshine and clay,
my one hand holding tight
my other hand; come celebrate
with me that everyday
something has tried to kill me
and has failed.

—Lucille Clifton

ACT V

White Complicity & Performative Wokeness

Uncomfortable White Friend (A Poem)

I shake you up
Wake you up
Disrupt you
Interrupt you
Pierce you
Re-steer you
Turning you into
Excuse-less
Time to get purpose-full
So go ahead
Be annoyed
Be irritated
Be angry
Be sure...
You know
the WHY of your unsettling
Sit with it
Intuit it
Let it stir you
Unfurl in you
Mold you
Unfold in you
Equip you
To fix it
To remix it
Till ev'rybody gets it

—\o/ tmr

Their Silence Ain't Golden

Silence was always part of the contract. Let me go back a bit and explain. Racialization is the arbitrary historical grouping of people according to our skin color and skin tones. It became a tool to justify the cruel treatment of non-white people.

Racialization was the close forerunner to white supremacy. It morphed into colonialism, slavery, and Jim Crow laws whereby the overriding principle or belief is that people of certain races or skin color are fundamentally different and therefore deserve their treatment.

How do you get humans to treat other humans inhumanely? Convince them that "other humans" aren't human. How do you convince them that we're not human? Dehumanize us through enslavement whereby we are stripped of our language, cul-ture, dignity, family.

Raped and then bred like animals.

"You can't blame us for what our ancestors did."

That's what they like to say.

And yeah, we know what else they like to say—"not all white people." I'll borrow this go-to deflection phrase to say this. Though not all white people actively participate, their inherited learned racism and safety from mistreatment led them to commit one of their biggest sins.

SILENCE.

Their silence is one of the biggest threats to us and loudest killers of us. Just because white folks can assuage their guilt when they don't themselves pull the trigger or when it's not their knee on our necks means nothing. Their silence makes them willing accomplices to any and all assaults on our lives and well-being. Full stop.

After their May 25 shock, they're going quiet again. It's been happening gradually. Have you noticed? It didn't take long, did it? Murders don't ever get old in the Black community. We remember. We carry all of them.

Killings are not what we wanna be talking about, but our "say their name" hashtags are for white folks' knowledge not ours. For us, it's a matter of honor and tribute mixed with outrage, not knowledge. If we don't keep the killings of Black bodies forefront in white folks' consciousness and make it a part of the oral record at minimum, then they get to normalize the horrors they perpetuate. Not letting them forget the threats that take the lives of Black bodies is critically important for our safety and survival so that they don't grow numb and hardened to this year's murders, like they've grown hard to the rest.

It's been more than six months since those 8 minutes and 46 seconds rocked the world. I could never bring my eyes to watch George Floyd's suffering and killing, nor could I bring my mother's ears to hear him calling out for his mother. I only know because of the reports. My heart continues to swell with mother's grief thinking about that. Those cries of a dying man for his mother. His murder and "that" utterly broke me.

"Mama" tugs at me hard. I'm a mama of two adult children— one who still calls me "mommy," and both who could be killed while Black. So, my "regular" blaxhaustion and this "new" blaxhaustion since May 25 have me occupying a new emotional space. I refer to my before-trump life, my before-covid life (BC), and now my before-George Floyd's murder life.

A world of witnesses to his murder. It appears that time flies when you do nothing. And that's what many white folks have done—nothing.

NOTHING.

Like so many of us, I've been paying attention to which companies and their leadership have reverted to business as usual.

Where's the substantive change and the progress to show for their grand rush to publicly claim their commitment to our lives and our well-being?

So many were and still are writing checks their ass can't cash, talking out the side of their necks, tryin' us. But we know. Black women always know. And if people had listened to us in 2016, we would not be where we are today with the worst of whiteness and whiteness disciples on proud and blatant display.

Oh wait...my mind is shifting to that other period in U.S. history that this country has never fully acknowledged or for which it has never atoned. Reckoning, payback, and karma have conflated and presents us with this twisted existence that white folks are bound by and bound to.

Justice is coming.

In the meantime, we get to hear them break their silence with dumb shit like this –

"I didn't own slaves."
"I wasn't even alive then."
"I'm not responsible for what my ancestors did."
"That was another time, another generation."
"It's not my fault what was done back then."

Statements like these prove that they still haven't done the work of educating themselves. If they did, they'd know that when they reap the benefits of a white supremacist system that elevates whiteness and do nothing about the costs to the lives of the oppressed, they also own all the liabilities of the harm and damage.

Their benefits have been ongoing, and they've welcomed and taken full advantage of whiteness perks.

Our damages have been ongoing, and we've suffered life-endangering and life-ending racism in every space we navigate. Insert a 3-syllable clap here—E VE RY space.

White folks don't get to conveniently pick and choose their ignorance or innocence. They don't get to confidently participate in collective selective amnesia. They don't get to comfortably claim individual freedom from culpability.

They own this.

They need to stop deflecting to "those other white people" who wear white sheets and carry guns, and step up to make things right.

The enabling good white folks are the ones really killing us.

What a Privilege

Privilege.

Another term that upsets them. Boo-hoo.

Privilege for them involves getting to choose when and where they want to take a stand.

Privilege for them is knowing that they and their humanity are safe.

Privilege for them is the power to determine and judge if there is a need for protest or confrontation.

Privilege for them is the freedom to decide whether to take on the discomfort or inconvenience of speaking up.

I was asked a question by a white man who had been unsettled by something I wrote. He reached out to me with a question, and I provided him with this answer. When you read my response, I'm sure you'll know what question I'm answering that we're ALWAYS answering.

"The pain of having no one speak up is oftentimes greater—much greater. For instance, when 'nigger bitch' was screamed at me in a public space, it was in clear earshot of

many people. Whenever I re-live that painful incident, it's the averted gazes and the silence of every single person who witnessed it that remain etched in my memory. Nobody said a word. Not to me. Not to the spewer of hate. That's what I remember most. That's what hurts the most. There is no defense of innocent bystanders whose comfort gets to be prioritized over my pain. There are no innocent bystanders in a world full of hate and bigotry."

If—IF—white folks were really serious about being anti-racist and dismantling racism, they would've already abandoned their self-deception and their self-proclaimed entitlement of ease and comfort for a commitment to do the work.

Instead though, they excuse and minimize the racism of family and friends. "But Aunt Betty doesn't really mean anything by it" or "Grandpa Bob is harmless."

No. Betty does mean something by it.

And no. Grandpa Bob is harmful.

White folks are what they tolerate—in themselves and in their family members.

Meanwhile, 2020 keeps serving up surprises.

There's a new app called "PulledOver," which more easily records interactions with police when folks get pulled over and is equipped to instantly share the footage to social media. Guess which demographic it's mostly marketed to? Hmph.

Privilege is NOT needing new and innovative strategies for not getting killed.

Privilege is NOT having random thoughts about where to source a personal bodycam for civilian use...you know...as a backup...just in case...

Those ones the pattyrollers wear seem to have a conveniently malfunctioning on-off switch.

Did one of my sistahs just call "Bingo"?

Window Dressing Poltergeist Style

Do you remember that *Poltergeist* movie from the early 1980's? Do you remember that famous climactic scene in which the dad realized what his boss had done when all those dead bodies came rupturing up through the floor in his house?

By way of a general summary, I'll give you the highlights. The company that the dad worked for wanted to plow ahead and build this new thing without dealing with the stuff that was necessary to deal with. Instead of going about it the right way, the company took a short-cut that was more expedient and more profitable: they simply ignored the stuff as if it didn't exist. In the end, the stuff cropped up and destroyed the new thing and devastated lives in the process.

There are many performative companies out here doing it *Poltergeist* style. To loosely borrow from the dad's line to his boss, "You changed the window dressing, but you left the racism, didn't you?!? You son-of-a-bitch, you left the racism, and you only changed the window dressing! You! Only! Changed! The! Window! Dressing! Why?!? Why?!?"

So now for the details. In the movie, a development company built a new housing development on the land of a bull-dozed cemetery that was leveled for the purposes of "progress" and "expansion." In the spirit of greed and entitlement and absent any proper and solemn preparation and procedures, the company only relocated the headstones to another piece of land but didn't relocate the dead bodies. The dead bodies in essence became the foundation upon which an entire brand-new housing development was built.

It's the same with organizations that think they can hire a Black Chief Diversity Officer and hire some Black folks to make the company look inclusive but haven't done a thing to address the racism they're bringing Black folks into. A presto-chango in representation for the sake of appearance does not do any-thing if a company has not addressed the racism within the organization and within themselves.

Window dressing is the euphemistic equivalent of applying band-aids. And it's the seasonal one-off of the moment. "What is the quickest thing we can do right now to make ourselves look better?" Companies have shown us that this question was the overriding impetus for what we know are mere performative acts.

Transformation, on the other hand, requires the ongoing work and results from constant unlearning, learning, relearning. Rinse. Repeat. Without doing the work, the rot of racism resurfaces. And from there it's all bad.

Just like the *Poltergeist* movie boss learned, there is no secret sauce, no short cuts. No quick anti-racism or DEI strategy. It's called work for a reason. Bottom line is that we are so over it with companies slapping a DEI window dressing or window sticker on top of existing racism and then parading it out to us and luring us into an environment in which our psychological and emotional safety are threatened. As far as I'm concerned, when companies pull that shit, it's premeditated racism.

> **Janeisha Cambridge** here, and I'm Speaking. You, Black woman, were taught to be twice as good and work twice as hard. When you speak, you command authority and exude purpose. Don't let anyone make you question if you deserve to be in that space. You are not an imposter.

Whiteness Preservation System™ (WPS)

WPS is what she meant by "fragility." WPS is what white folks are feeling and then calling it "discomfort."

If white folks were to stop projecting and deflecting and really look inward and ask themselves the important questions yet to be answered, we'd finally be having the long overdue conversations that we're meant to have.

- Why is Black Lives Mater triggering to their WPS?
- Why do anti-racism and DEI in the workplace feel like "reverse discrimination? (Is there a "right" way to discriminate?)
- Why do racial equity and justice feel unfair?
- Why does the rejection of confederate artifacts and heroes seem un-American?
- Why does the "firing" of Aunt Jemima and Uncle Ben appear extreme?
- Why do calls for police reform and accountability seem to go overboard?

White supremacy is not the only thing to be dismantled. There is much introspective head-work and heart-work that must accompany it. Changes to systems, practices, policies that do not include self-transformation spell only *Poltergeist*-style window-dressing.

> **DeAnnah Stinson Reese** here, and I'm speaking. I am not here to pacify your ego or to make you feel good. I am here to bring conviction that will prompt change. The same glass ceiling that tries to keep me from growing too much, is the same glass floor that keeps you from falling too far. So I'm here to fight for what's mine.

Normal Fuh Who?

Have you been listening to all THEIR tone-deaf calls for "normal" and a return to "normal"? Have you also noticed how many of US are not calling for the kind of normal that white folks are longing for?

Their normal of pre-covid, pre-Ahmaud Arbery, pre-Breonna Taylor, pre-George Floyd, and pre-Amy Cooper is just their whiteness preservation system (WPS) trying to reset itself to its original whiteness factory settings.

Normal for them ain't never been normal for us.

Going back to pre-2020 racism is a big hell no.

Going back to pre-2016 racism is a big hell no.

Going back to yesterday is a big hell no.

How about white folks get off their complicit asses and work to achieve a safe and healthy normal for everybody for the first time?!

Cuz there ain't a damn place or time in this country that Black folks can go back to!

I'm Not Going Back to Normal (A Poem)

It's a "No"
Unh uh

There's No Way

No
No
No
Noooo Way!

Iiiiiiiiii'm NOT
Goooo-ing BACK
To
A
Normal that doesn't
Respect
Promote
Listen
Nor protect
My
Carmel, mocha, chocolate
Skin

In fact

Normal proved itself deadly harmful dangerous & whack to my Black

Skin

It
Has
Been
That
"Normal"

That kills & still

Makes
Us
Sick
There's No Way

No
No
No
Noooo Way!

Iiiiiiiiiii'm NOT
Goooo-ing BACK
To

Normal that
Doesn't
Work

That keep
A jerk

On
Pains it projects
And questions
When I say & speak to generational medical experimentation
Pain

Still not acknowledged
Now still holding us hostage
Dr. Sims perfected his art
Cutting out our parts

They dare not speak
To the open secret
That plays
On repeat

No...unless something far better is created
That tells the tale promoting
my melanated
skin
I'm not going
Back
to the place folk call
'normal'
it's still too harmful
Create somethin' new
Yeah you'll see me there
With my Crown in my hair
So...Let's simply do
That
Part
Anything lesser
Is a far greater
Danger
to me, us and we
And our parts

— Teddi Williams

She Been 'Bout Ta Lose Her Job

It's been a long time coming. Aunt Jemima, the face of a brand, is unemployed after years of faithful service. Yeah, I know about Uncle Ben, too, but I'm focusing on HER right now. And yeah, again, the word at the breakfast table is Mrs. Butterworth is gettin' nervous.

Well listen, Quaker Oats and those other corporations claim they are starting to get a clue that caricature isn't what we had in mind with "representation matters."

Oh pleez! The stereotypical roots of Aunt Jemima were long known by Quaker Oats, who continued to capitalize on the mammy stereotype even through iterations of modernizing her to stay current with the times.

They knew. Feigning innocence to save face (no pun intended) is a punk-ass performative move. Their sudden epiphany of moral clarity and racial justice is merely a profit response by Quaker Oats.

Again, I can't stress this enough, they knew.

That it takes well over 100 years to get to this point of social responsibility when we were all along pointing out harmful images and icons. Yeah, they knew. What Quaker Oats is experiencing is a sudden case of social justice conscience, a condition felt only in their profit followed by bouts of publicly induced showings of "remorse and regret."

Tradition and systemic racism are interchangeable. That's why folks will dig in their heels and hang on to it until it disrupts their profit.

In this climate of Black Lives Matter, companies can't afford the bad PR and bad optics risk of an economic boycott, which spells bad news for the brand.

Money talks and walks. Aunt Jemima was good for them until she wasn't. No word if she or the family was adequately compensated or received a cut of the profits over the years.

Our Black lives may not matter, but this is a reminder that our Black dollars do. For both companies and individuals, gain or loss of profit is a great motivator for change. Appeals to decency and morality, not so much.

The Show Needs Actors

Why do we continue to celebrate the symbolic elevation of us into name-only high-level DEI positions of power without holding us accountable for making a difference for us?

We keep celebrating and applauding "the first one of us" when companies use one of us to make themselves look like they are doing what they should have been doing all along. Hiring their "first this" or their "first that" is nothing to celebrate. And quite frankly, it's insulting and racist.

"Oh look, we got ourselves a good one, our first. Look at us. We're an inclusive and progressive company. We support BLM."

Oh pleeeezzzz.

Once the newness of the announcement wears off, we rarely if ever hear about what these folks are doing. How are they changing the recruiting process? What have they done to increase the hiring of Black folks? How are they impacting the advancement opportunities for Black employees? Have they worked to increase sponsors for underrepresented and marginalized employees? What real efforts have they put into achieving pay equity within the company? Are they just drawing a paycheck, or are they using their position to advance anti-racism, inclusion, and belonging?

I can no longer be satisfied with receiving nothing but emotional satisfaction when one of our own lands what should be an empowered position. Just like we evaluate companies, we have to also evaluate our folk on what they do and don't do. I want to hear that they are making waves and disrupting versus lickin' white boots. Cuz if they ain't doin' nothin' but lickin' boots, they are a threat.

> **Emeline Mugisha** here, and I'm speaking. As a radical truth-teller, I've never seen a white-dominated space in Amerikkka that emboldens the Black woman and her voice rather than preferring to boogie. Boogying is what helps maintain the status quo that tells us to tone it down. No, thank you. I'm not here for the nonsense. I'm here to lead and to live—undaunted, unshakeable, and unshackled.

As for the companies themselves that parade and publicly display their new acquisitions as if they are prized purchases from the auction block, they ain't fooling us at all. Again, we see right through stuff.

At the same time though, the clock is way beyond just ticking. Companies have had more than enough time to do the real work if they wanted to. Many have chosen instead to perfect their performative stance with a cast of actors that includes a token Black in a non-starring ancillary role in the big house. In other words, they've committed to change out the curtains but leave the white supremacy structure intact.

It was the easier route for the company, but it has in no way appeased us or lessened the threats we face at work. We know the difference between a show and a real commitment. Real commitment doesn't let covid, a remote workforce, layoffs, and budget cuts keep them from BLM, equity, inclusion, and belonging. Again, as the saying goes, companies and company leaders rushed to write a check with their lips that their ass couldn't cash by either hiring Black DEI figure-heads or promoting from within someone to be their Black DEI figure-head.

The inaction of these actors is not all on them. We know about the puppet strings and muzzles. No one can be an effective champion for anti-racism, equity, or inclusion when they're "forcibly" tompromised by companies that

bind them

shackle them

censor them

disempower them

defund them

and don't all-in support them.

When these actors are failing—and many of them are—it's more so the company's failure. Oh wait...it's more accurate to say that it's the company's win. Cuz when power wants something to happen or not happen,

Power. Makes. It. Happen.

That includes making the DEI actor the patsy for DEI failure while the company and its white leadership take the win for maintaining the status quo of white supremacy.

Yeah, when the Chief Diversity Officer got fired, we saw what they did there.

They Put on Quite a Show

When they know better, they still don't do better. However, they want to publicly claim better so that they appear better without doing the work. Hmph.

It's all merely performative PR posturing in the "age" of Black Lives Matter.

What they're doing is saying the right things to distract from them not doing anything substantive.

Companies are doing it.

Individuals are doing it.

I'm watching the shit-show, sister, and also channeling my inner Rihanna.

> *"You put on quite a show*
> *Really had me goin'*
> *But now it's time to go*
> *Curtain's finally closin'*
> *That was quite a show*
> *Very entertaining*
> *But it's over now."*

When they know better, they double-down. We knew it'd be a limited run. Nothing to see here. Show's over.

> **Dr. Sarah Blair-Reid** here, and I'm speaking. I am a Black woman; my life is valid. The colour of my skin does not devalue my knowledge or qualifications. Do not ask a white man to repeat my words because you don't deem my voice worth your attention. Listening to me isn't an exercise in Diversity and Inclusion. We're tired, we're rising up; a reckoning is coming.

Truths, Lies, and No Videotape

Ironically, it's only the blatant spewers of hate who are usually caught on camera.

But what about all the instances we don't get to see?

Our word has never been good enough no matter how many of us are saying the same word.

Positively Neo-Racist

Positive psychology with its truisms and platitudes is often a source of tremendous threat. Bearing the fruit of what sounds like innocent positivity, it is insidious in what it pushes.

Take for example a white male social media influencer who preaches to his followers that "… the problem in society these days, is that people tend to forget that nobody can offend you, unless you choose to be offended. And when you choose to be offended, you've basically handed over your power."

Sounds innocent enough…right? Wrong. This is known as a type of subtle racist ideology that is hard to prove and will likely be met with gaslighting and claims of us loving to "play the victim."

Additionally, the entire belief that "nobody can offend you unless you choose to be offended" is a danger and threat to us who regularly experience psychological, emotional, and physical racial assaults. It is a belief that exonerates from re-sponsibility and accountability the perpetrators of anti-Black speech and behavior. It wrongfully places the blame on us for speaking out against our oppression.

In other words, blame the victim for being victimized.

Blame the oppressed for their oppression.

And punish us when we talk about it!

If we stayed silent, then our silence would be added to their silence. And all that silence makes the system thrive.

The Face of DivHERsity is Her

Diversity is not for us. It's for her. And that makes diversity a threat in the recruiting and hiring of Black folks. As the diversity elephant in the room, white women check the company's box for gender with the bonus of whiteness.

The hidden data in plain sight of our eyes reveals that white women are the primary beneficiaries of companies' diversity, equity, and inclusion initiatives, and companies will tout their diversity numbers to include white women in order to distract from a lack of racial diversity.

So we know exactly what it means for a company to be committed to DEI. That's why it's critical to keep the focus on anti-Black racism and non-Black POC racism. Anti-Black racism is what brings us and non-Black POC back into the conversation.

> **Monique Braham-Evans** here, and I'm speaking. While you may not think I have something worthy to say because I don't belong here and must be a diversity hire—you're wrong. I actually am qualified and work twice as hard just to prove that. So when words start to pour from my mouth, don't overtalk me because you choose to overlook my people. Be respectful.

Them Bitches Stole Anti-Racism

Speaking of anti-racism, white women are being prioritized and hired for anti-racism work instead of Black voices being hired to advance anti-racism work.

White women are stealing from Black anti-racism educators under the guise of approaching us with fake sisterhood and collaboration.

White women are cashing in and profiting off of our thought leadership and content.

White women are using the Black Lives Matter hashtag as a money-maker to center themselves at the expense of our Black lives and voices.

Again, the visual data is quite compelling and reveals that though both white men and white women are educating folks on racism, it is white women—I repeat, white women—who have clearly established a niche for themselves in this space, doing what white women always do—inserting themselves in a space and taking up all the room whether they should be in the space or not.

Black women anti-racism educators who work independently often compete with white women. The less "mainstream" we are and the less uncomfortable we make white folks, the less frequently we are hired. And the per-formative companies who are only looking for the appearance of anti-racism and inclusion are famous for hiring white women and white-owned companies to teach their employees about racism.

The major take-away is that whiteness is profiting from both racism and anti-racism. And Black women are the hidden figures primarily impacted. It's been a standard practice to not pay us for our intellectual property or for our thought leadership. It's also been a standard practice to underpay us. White folks who are whitesplaining anti-racism get compensated at higher rates!

Black women, in particular, are sought out to provide advice and pointers, to serve on committees, to lead BRGs, to speak at conferences, to smooth things over with other Black employees, to contribute to the diversity newsletter, to teach white folks, to be the token at company events, etc.

FOR FREE!

NO PROFFER OF CASH MONEY!

The caucacity never ends.

Just like the 'Rona exposed what was already there, anti-racism has exposed the continued devaluing of Black women. We are frequently expected by whiteness to offer up our labor for free. Anecdotal and quantitative data bear out that this happens to Black women more than to any other demographic.

Companies that rely on white educators and white owned companies are not modeling that our lives matter when they outsource "Black matters" to whiteness. They are perpetuating the system whereby white folks—and those who identify as white—benefit while Black folks remain disenfranchised. There is no way a person, corporation, leader or etc. can say they are serious about anti-racism when they hire a white voice to guide them through the process!

And again, it's mostly white women who are building businesses and profiting from being anti-racism educators and trainers. Anti-racism for many is mere performance art, and they are good at performing. Many of them have no idea what they are doing and reach out to steal thought leadership from Black women.

"Can I pick your brain?"
"I'd like to get your thoughts on…"
"I'm looking forward to learning from you."
"Can you walk us through your process?"
"Can we set up a call to see if you could help us?"
"The team would like to meet with you for an hour to better understand your methods."

The end result is that our labor is stolen, and the theft leads to profit and prestige for the thief.

Sound familiar?

Slavery 5.0. Or whatever version we're currently on.

Seriously, I can't even with white women.

They keep finding ways to be one of our biggest threats.

White Women Are So Extra

With all the talk this year from white folks about their freedom and protecting their freedom from infringement, I find myself asking this question over and over again, "What about our freedom?"

On this day in particular as we recognize and celebrate Juneteenth, I'm reflecting on my desire to be free of entitled white women that think my sole purpose in life is to serve them. I'm talking about Karen who, when I refused to give her the answer and instead told her to do the work, said this to me: "This isn't how you help us learn. It just isn't."

Girl, hold up...

That's pretty much how my second round with her went when she realized that she had gone and messed with the wrong one. Use your vivid imagination for that first round.

First off, she and I fundamentally disagreed. She calls herself a supporter. I'm calling her a Karen. Noticeably absent pre-May 25, she is now interested to learn and demanded that I teach her.

Now that she is interested to learn, she demanded that I thank her for her interest and willingness.

Now that she is interested to learn, she demanded that I center her feelings and make things easy for HER!

There are

not enough slow breaths I can breathe in,

not enough weight in a 1 to 10 count,

not enough "Jesus, please help me" energy,

not enough willpower to release this tension...

for me to manage through this fresh new wave of ignorance that has accompanied their awakening. All of a sudden, they, who have participated in and benefited from racism, want us to drop everything and teach them about racism!

White women take up nearly every damn square on our bingo card.

At this point, sistahs, why do we even bother putting on earrings?

I mean that metaphorically, of course, but guurrlll, you do you. I get it. And I ain't judging y'all.

An Actual Apology from a White Man

"I am sorry to all the POC who are having to defend their emotions, views, perceptions, and beliefs to white folks who challenge everything you have to say.

I am sorry that you have to exist in a society where your trauma, fear and frustration is met with "Well have you thought about how white people feel?" and "Two wrongs don't make a right!" comments.

I am sorry that you have to see over and over the racist terms and "jokes" that have existed for decades being excused because of the fragility of white folks.

I am sorry that people make you explain why their words have hurt you, as if they are oblivious to the fight against racism that your community built on their own.

And I am sorry that in 2020, we have the technology and capability to utilize a platform to help spread the voices and messages of an under-represented, oppressed and silenced population, but instead of embracing your truth if we agree or moving on if we don't, we instead decide to attempt to demoralize, insult and dismiss your words.

I am ashamed. "

This is the apology posted to me by a white man after he OBSERVED that I was being attacked by enraged white folks.

He had no direct words for the attackers and failed to address them head-on.

I wonder how long after the acknowledgment and apology stages does it take to advance to the action stage?

Oh wait...never mind.

A Charge of Professionalism Ain't NO Compliment

"I appreciate your professionalism, Theresa." Comments like this make me suspect, especially when they come from white folks.

I start questioning myself because as we know, there's not just one definition of professionalism. There's the one, according to Merriam-Webster's Dictionary, that simply points to the "exhibition of courteous, conscientious, and generally business-like conduct in the workplace."

Okay, fine, that sounds all well and good. I'll take it. But the other definition involves a professionalism ascribed to us when we sacrifice our sense of emotional and psychological safety so that white comfort and safety can be prioritized. That latter part of the definition that centers them is their focus. They want to feel like we are playing nice. Appeasing and placating them.

What we're really doing is keeping our calm in the face of some straight-up foul racist nonsense. Like that time my Karen manager told me that I don't have the universal appeal for clients that white John has. Or that time my white co-facilitator complimented my handling of the white asshole participant who insisted my Ivy League education had to be courtesy of affirmative action.

Professionalism? Yeah, no.

Composure and restraint.

Plus, Black women tend to have a certain "oh hayell naw" energy about us that requires no articulated violation of white professionalism.

Dr. Janice Gassam Asare here, and I'm speaking. We are everything. Pure and unfiltered, in its rawest form. They see the unadulterated gold within us and want to duplicate it, take from it, bastardize it. Regardless of multiple attempts to remove our magic from the roots, we are the roses that grow from concrete and they cannot destroy us. Keep standing in your beauty. You are greatness personified.

BLM: Black Lives Monetized (A Poem)

it's trashy
to cash in
on Black skin

so shameful
disdainful
untasteful

their prize is to
capitalize
on Black lives

it's disgusting
no repercussions
only dollars
for their coffers

— \o/ tmr

Conditional Support from Fake Allies

As long as...

That's how they need to start every sentence so that it matches up with their fakery. The minute we call them on their own stuff, that automatic whiteness preservation system (WPS) kicks in. Then it's the deflection and the calling on their Black friends who can vouch for them. One self-professed white ally even had the caucacity to dismiss me by threatening me with his relationships with other Black folks who can vouch for him. "My Black friends disagree with you about me," he said to me. Whiteness using Black folks to shut down Black folks is a common racist tactic. He had outed himself as a fake.

> **CaJuana Capps** here, and I'm speaking. Keep your fake allyship. As a Christian, black and African-American woman, I reject whiteness, abuse, and evil racial aggressors. Racial inequality, inequity, and exclusion is NOT God's will. Racism is inhumane! My emotional health is NOT your punching bag. May God promote black women and destroy white supremacy in Jesus name, Amen.

Fakers and other "good people" are primarily concerned with the posturing that keeps them and whiteness centered. In addition to the dead give-away of name-dropping and constant reminders of their Black friends, these are the ones who profess to have been disgusted by the killing of George Floyd but are careful to refer to it as "George Floyd's death." Really?! No! He was MURDERED! I guess their shock and outrage at witnessing his on-camera murder had an expiration date.

What would it take for whiteness to come down from its pedestal and step outside of the house of cards white supremacy built and work on being actively anti-racist?

Of course I recognize that my question assumes that every human being is in possession of a moral compass. I keep forgetting that power and privilege rarely respond to moral appeals. Fake allies have built a brand as allies, so they have to keep up the persona to support their public image. Fake allies don't do well with realness when it comes to the racist stuff they carry, making their support limited and provisional at best. If realness and truth are upsetting to privileged white allies, they can never be a real support for us. They can never advance to accomplice. They are stuck in the "terms and conditions" game that fake allies play.

They are not looking to do the self-work. They are seeking in-name-only prestige. They want other "good" white folks to look at them and applaud them. *"Such good work you're doing for Black people. I hope they appreciate it and you."* The name they seek to make for themselves does not include them being corrected by Black women, because we exist outside of the safe narrative that blinds them to the realities of our life. Bottom line is that whiteness doesn't need to know us or our experiences because it doesn't have to. It's how the contract of whiteness works.

Sure. Their fake-ass support which they make conditionally available, is ours for the taking.

As long as we don't disagree with or challenge them.

As long as we don't upset their worldview.

As long *ass...*

Emphasis on (fake) ass...

10 Shades of Fake

1. Inability to de-center themselves. This has been an ongoing characteristic, and I must say that during the 'Rona era, this first one is on steroids and glaringly apparent. Per the usual, white women get an honorable mention on this one as they frequently prioritize their own needs and experiences over ours while exerting racial dominance. They've perfected their pivot from any talks about race to talks about gender and their quest for the power of patriarchy or for the power of proximity to it. They represent every threat their male counterparts represent—and more—except for that whole penis thing. They are beasts when it comes to emotional and psychological manipulation.

"You cannot expect your feelings to be the center of someone else's struggle...[S]ometimes it simply isn't your turn to be the focus of the conversation."

—Mikki Kendall

2. Defensiveness when they are corrected by us. Instead of using the correction as an opportunity to learn, white folks double down and mobilize all their energy to deflect and negate the correction by any means necessary. Often, they will crowd source other Black folks to shut us down, "See. These Black people agree with me and disagree with you." They are driven by a whiteness preservation system (WPS) that will not allow them to concede to Blackness and give the impression that a Black person is more knowledgeable than they are and is better equipped to speak to certain issues.

3. Refusal to apologize when they mess up. *You got it all wrong. What I said is not racist. You're overreacting.* Both refusal and inability to apologize must be a part of the whiteness legacy: Never apologize. Never admit wrongdoing. Maybe they believe that when they do, they are liable for the impact and are obligated to make amends. Can this be the hold-up on reparations? But I digress. In short, white folks would rather go silent and separate themselves from us than apologize. Betty and Brad couldn't take the heat from the discomfort of their learning and unlearning missteps, so they moved on to nicer Black people likely to let them off the hook.

4. Race-splaining about us. I confess. This one should really be on a different list. 10 shades of Dumbass! Do they even realize how tone-deaf, caucacity-laden, and stupid this route is? When we get one of these, it's best to just walk away. Walk away fast before we say or do something we'll NEVER regret. Repeat a string of "help me Jesus, bless they lil' heart," and then move on. The white person that engages in race-splaining is best left to other white folks to deal with.

5. Prioritization of their own voice. They are quick with vocalizing their own claims, thoughts, and ideas instead of prioritizing their learning and unlearning. Because anti-racism is a business they want to capitalize on, their words and actions are designed to position themselves as influencers or experts for hire. They rarely if ever amplify our voices and will often co-opt our voices as their own.

6. The self-amplifying and self-elevating by flaunting and showboating receipts. *Yay me! Look at what I did. Look at what I'm doing. Look at what I will be doing.* If these kinds of exclamations and statements are all we ever hear from them, then they are in it just to be seen. These fakers are obsessed with proving their realness instead of actually being about the realness. They opt for "talk about it" versus "be about it." They are fake because their oxygen is affirmation and validation from others.

7. Expectation of gratitude more than an expectation of progress and change. Here they go with that savior complex! Their mindset is stuck on benevolence privilege. They want to be thanked and acknowledged for everything they say and do—no matter how inconsequential or how inappropriate. Hell, they even praise themselves. *Guess what? I watched 13th and convinced my (racist) parents to watch it, too. That was no easy feat to pull off because they're sensitive about that kind of subject matter.* Ugh. What do they want?! A noble whiteness of the moment trophy? Their empty words and gestures are directly proportional to the kudos and praise they receive. When the expressions of gratitude dry up, their pseudo-support also dries up.

8. Abandoning (ally)ship when their feelings get hurt. These fakers are magical. When their "fragile" feelings get hurt, they disappear in a hot white minute. Poof. Before they leave the show though and exit stage right, they manage to deliver a soliloquy and center themselves one last time. *I'm trying, and it never seems good enough. I always end up saying the wrong thing. I'm just going to not say anything anymore.* Boo-hoo. It doesn't matter if truth, feedback, or correction causes their negative reaction. These fakers don't have the staying power or the thick skin for anti-racism. They'd rather gather all their toys and storm out the room and will sometimes return quietly without owning up to or even acknowledging why they left in the first place. The only part of allying they do well is that lying part.

9. Picking and choosing when "allying" is convenient for them. These folks operate on a rationing system. They have a "wokeness quota." We can recognize them because they don't regard anti-racism work as ongoing and constant, and they operate on conveniently choosing from their menu of *easy, hard, or difficult* to determine when to speak up or act. They are the ones who when they determine that they've done or said something major, they can then reward themselves with a pass—one that allows them to let subsequent racism slide when they hear or see it. The question that these fakers always ask themselves is *How uncomfortable is this going to be for ME?*

10. Weaponizing their Black friends to shut us down when we call them on their shit. Again, these are fakers who collect Black tools to shut us down. They specialize in direct and indirect gaslighting. We'll know them by the Black company they keep. Though they surround themselves with Black company, very rarely do they amplify the voices of that Black company. What we see them doing is dispatching their Black company to silence other Black voices. *My Black friends agree with me, and they told me that I didn't say or do anything wrong.*

Here's the takeaway—Fakers are not our friends. They are a threat to us and to the real work of anti-Black racism.

Top 10 Hits that Cut

These are the hits we constantly absorb that result in tiny cuts every time we hear them from clueless white folks. The cumulative impact of being dismissed and minimized over and over again cannot be underestimated for the toll it takes on our psyche and on our emotional and mental energy. We experience fatigue quicker, and we feel frustration deeper.

In short, it's hella stressful to be Black.

It's hella blaxhausting to be a Black woman!

Fuh real!

1. **"All lives matter."** (Me: Where the hell was "all lives matter" from 1619 to 2020? Nowhere. This phrase is a hypocritical reactionary lie. An illogical and emotional piece of propagandist white bullshit, at best.)

2. **"Not all white people."**

3. **"I've been discriminated against, too."** (Me: Like that time they lost that promotion from vice president to senior vice president because of their Boston accent. Yeah, that's just like racism. Cue my eye-roll.)

4. **"My** [they insert a relationship that they think somehow exonerates or excuses them from being racist] **is Black."**

5. **"I don't see color."** (Me: They sure as hell see it during the job interview! And unlike actual color-blindness, racial color-blindness is not a medical condition; it's an ignorant condition.)

6. **"We're all human."**

7. **"I experienced the same thing when..."** (Me: They fixate on a one-time event that doesn't even come close to being the same but insist on centering themselves anyway.)

8. **"Racism goes both ways."** (Me: Oh here they go with that gaslighting "reverse racism" crap.)

9. **"Plenty of Black people have privilege."** (Me: A favorite go-to of theirs is engaging in whataboutism that conflates race with socioeconomic status, education, etc.)

10. **"This might sound racist BUT..."** or **"I hope this doesn't come off as racist BUT..."** (Me: For the love of all that is Holy, why don't they ever choose the "don't say it then" option?! Just don't fuckin' say it!)

When I hear any of this, I immediately start praying for the person, "please, just stop talking, please." Praying is better than a laying on of hands. Plus, can't do that because of covid.

With these 10 hits, let's not miss the big picture of what whiteness is and does.

Whiteness revels in its largeness and in its declaration of its right-ness in all things.

Whiteness acts like the only child among 9 siblings.

Whiteness takes its turn and then justifies having everybody else's turn, too.

Whiteness claims expertise on our unique experiences of oppression.

Whiteness pushes a narrative that it has no business pushing.

Whiteness stays entitled.

And what do we do? We waste our energy proving the basics that need no proving. We major in the "minors" and thus contribute to our own blaxhaustion. I know. Lord, help me. Help *us*.

> **Alisha C. Gray** here, and I'm speaking. We're here to serve our purposes NOT dull our shine, tiptoe around much less make you comfortable. Your privilege, entitlement, passive aggression proves your ignorance, hatred and fear of us and our power. To my beautiful melanated Kings and Queens: keep supporting each other, operating as the royalty we are; leading, teaching, covering, guiding, nurturing, inspiring… with love. ¡Poder Negro!

White supremacy is neither based on science or truth. It is based solely on the ability of a people in power to dominate and oppress other peoples. That's it. Nothing more.

White supremacy declared that we were 3/5 human and had it written in the U.S. Constitution as part of the official record of this country. Many of us are still proving our humanity in 2020. I admit that I was spinning my wheels, too, proving it. But once I made the decision to not debate my humanness, it helped. I've redirected that energy to focusing on the in-humanity of whiteness and of those who worship it.

I'd rather spotlight leaders who fail to declare the killings of Black bodies as a human rights crisis and who fail to condemn hate groups as the murdering domestic terrorists they are. I don't need to debate on Black Lives Matter. The fact that it's even been subject to debate, dismissal, and denial is a revelation to the world. Well, at least the parts of the world that are capable of seeing and listening.

> **Alana M. Hill** here, and I'm speaking. I have so much to teach you, but I need you to be quiet long enough. Learning comes after listening, and if you don't respect me enough to listen, I won't waste my energy worrying if you will learn. My life, education, and experience as a Black woman will teach you something if you just listen! You gon' learn today!

The myth of inferiority that whiteness worshippers project on us is exactly that – a myth they perpetuate in order to boost themselves up. That all the tenets of white supremacy spread from generation to generation makes it more aligned with a sick and twisted pyramid scheme than with anything legitimate.

Ain't No Party Like a White-Crashed Party

The recent awakening of "good" white folks to anti-Back racism after the murder of George Floyd is analogous to them arriving 400+ years late to a house-warming party which they claimed was too loud.

And bringing with them a cheap bottle of wine.

And expecting the host to explain, "Where is everybody?"

And insisting on pushing their way inside.

And taking a seat in the best seat in the house.

And after all of this, they wait for the host to uncork and serve them the wine with no regard for whether they are welcomed or not.

> **Sommer Sibilly-Brown** here, and I'm speaking. My lived experience qualifies me to lead in my community. I do not need your approval. This is my seat, a matter of fact this is my table and all the people who seem to think otherwise, this is your notice. My community is my domain. You do not determine our destiny. That is between us, our legacy, and God.

It is the picture of clueless whiteness unable or unwilling to shed their centered entitlement. And this ain't the kinda party where they can just show up fashionably late.

So, yeah. They best keep their "I didn't know it was this bad." Not enough of them fessing up to WHY – why didn't they know? Zero white folks in my circle have talked to me about this piece specifically. Of course that would require too much uncomfortable introspection. They are more comfortable ver-bally expressing "support" or "sympathy." The last time I checked—five minutes ago—support and sympathy don't keep Black folks safe or alive.

Whether it's silence or utterances of disbelief, I'm too busy thinking about how my family and I will stay safe, healthy, and alive. Sometimes I feel like we'd be better off locking ourselves in our proverbial house and denying them entrance when they come knocking. The downside though is that they can't slide underneath our door that bottle of wine they brought!

Buh-Bye Brad

Brad. You know him. We all know him. He's the white male self-professed ally who inserts himself into Black spaces to advise us on the negative impact on white folks of terms such as

228

"white people" and "white supremacy." Brad achieves this by treating us to a tone-deaf lecture on how the use of certain terms is counter-productive to our cause.

You know how it goes. His lecture starts with "not all white people" and ends in the place of no return—that we should be so grateful for white people who support our cause.

Not all white people, Theresa. And you risk losing so many of us who support you when you say that.

Sure, Brad. I'll hop right on correcting that. NEVER.

Whew. So many Brads out there. And they fit the profile. They fit the description. (Shout-out credit to modern-day pattyrollers for this language.)

Brad's objections to actual white supremacy, racism, etc. are not nearly as strong as his objections to the terms themselves.

Brad is against police brutality and killing of Black bodies, but he is for policing our voices and our tone.

Brad has never called out white folks for their racist speech or behavior, but touts how much he and his people have done for "the Black people." That "ingrate" language he uses is historically coded language and born of the same oppressors' sentiment pitched to our ancestors that they should be grateful to be slaves and thus be taken care of.

Brad is patronizing and considers us his "pet" project to teach and correct.

Brad is triggered by the centering of Black lives or our lived experiences, and his hurt manifests in a thinly veiled passive-aggressive high-road blessing pronounced on those of us who clap back.

Beware.

Brads are bad for us.

The minute they verbalize their feathers getting ruffled, they betray themselves. Bless they lil' heart.

Unconscious Bias is Fragility's Sibling

We can confidently say that 2020 offered "good" white folks the gift of acknowledging that they are all conscious now. No excuses. So it goes without saying that they should be having a white moment and moving past unconscious bias training.

Unconscious bias perpetuates the white fragility narrative and enables it at the same time. Unconscious bias training is optics driven and is usually favored by individuals and companies with performative initiatives that scratch the surface of DEI and bury anti-racism in a footnote to DEI.

Simply put, unconscious bias training does not address the implicit and explicit anti-Black racism that we face.

Unconscious bias training is not enough.

Unconscious bias training is exclusionary.

Unconscious bias training is insulting.

> **Erika M. Di Renzo** here, and I'm speaking. I remember growing up and rarely seeing myself in the world. Then came Vanessa Williams—now Kamala Harris. I don't even have words! To know that at "every" election your Human Rights and Humanity are dissected before courts. And now WE as Black Women made "this" happen. I've said it many, many times. The Magic of Black Women is endless.

"Good" White Folks Are the Dangerous Ones

Venita Stewart-Wilson here, and I'm speaking.
Consider the paradox of corporate America. A white
male hiring manager says, "...I thought HBCUs were for
people who couldn't get into real universities." I, an
HBCU executive grad, respond with, "Excuse me?" The
paradox of a successful HBCU grad is "What the fuck?"
OR to educate the ignorant?

Just like I can be a nice person with a kind spirit and still tell Karen to fuck-off when necessary, white folks can be "good" and still say and do racist stuff. Not strictly mutually exclusive concepts for them to grasp. I draw a line in the sand though with white folks who've decided that racism is not a dealbreaker for them. That's a problem. One I can't get over or dismiss because we

work *with* "good" white folks
work *for* "good" white folks
work *under* "good" white folks
fraternize *with* "good" white folks
are hired *by* "good" white folks
are promoted *by* "good" white folks
are evaluated *by* "good" white folks.

They are everywhere we have to be. Literally.

Future Cain here, and I'm speaking. People are experiencing white fragility because they have compromised their own consciousness. All my life I have been living a compromised lifestyle to make others feel comfortable with all the beautiful pieces of my intersectionality. Now is the time for others to embrace uncomfortableness, show empathy, be self-aware, and reflect in order to move humanity forward for all. Nuff said!

"We can disagree and still love each other unless your disagreement is rooted in my oppression and denial of my humanity and right to exist."
—James Baldwin

Good white folks. They think racism should be carried out in a more dignified manner. When we strip away guns, power, money, education, and "social refinement," we still have a match. Racism. Distinctions without a difference. Still racism.

Good white folks. They routinely explain away and rationalize racism by making it our fault and insisting that we must have done something to deserve the treatment we got. Even if they acknowledge a racist comment or incident, they tell us that it wasn't actually all that bad or tell us that we have to learn to put it all behind us and move on.

Good white folks. They tell us to let it go without addressing the issues causing our pain. They advise and instruct us on fixing our feelings rather than initiating and actively engaging in self-examination and self-transformation.

Good white folks. They tell us what is and is not racist and what the impact of racism is. *I don't believe that was racist; it just didn't sound racist to me. Are you sure you just didn't take it the wrong way?*

Good white folks. They take well-deserved time off when they get too tired of hearing about racism and step back into the comfort of whiteness to refuel themselves, leaving us to fight against and fend off assaults on our Blackness.

Good white folks. They wish us a "good evening" and "nice weekend" as if their words of platitude can guarantee our safety and survival until they see us again. Breonna Taylor's white colleagues, as they departed work for the safety of their homes, likely wished Breonna a "nice night" before she was shot in her home in the middle of the night.

Good white folks. They think we "exaggerate" or "make too much" of things. They secretly "believe" that if we would just not mention racism so much then things would be so much better for us. They think racism might go away if people stopped talking about it. Like a miracle. Who, sisters, wants to remind them that this head-in-the-sand strategy didn't work for the covid pandemic, and it won't work for the racism pandemic either?

They Wanna Play the "Get Out of Racism Free" Card

"I can't be racist."
"My best friend is Black."
"My wife/husband is Black."
"My children are Black."

White folks put so much energy into trying to convince us that they're not racist and hardly any energy into fighting against and dismantling racism itself. It's like they are looking for absolution or something. They think that if they can convince one of us, then they get a special stamp on their whiteness membership card. *"But Theresa says I'm not racist."*

Do they get a cookie from other white folks when they get one of us to sign off on their delusion? Instead of doing the work of anti-Black racism, the folks who traffic in touting their Black relationships betray how not far along they are on their journey.

And if we play the race card like they accuse us of doing, then how come after 400+ years of playing, none of us has ever pulled a "get out of racism free" card for ourselves? Huh? Where can we get one of those stamps? Cuz I'll stand in line for that stamp. All damn day if I have to. *"John certifies that Theresa is exempt from racism."*

Who's stacking our deck with a surplus of cards that say *"go to jail, go straight to jail, do not pass go, do not collect $200"*? We're not doing so well at these cards we play, so I wanna speak to a manager.

Before "gaslighting" became a popular term, we were intimately familiar with it. Our calls to the manager about our racist treatment were never prioritized like Karen's calls to the manager. Our calls have been met consistently with scorn and dismissal. Hell, we even got relegated to the bottom of the cue. And then after that, the manager changed the call number so we couldn't get through.

We do what we know how to do. When they don't and won't listen to us, we speak words of support and assurance to the me inside. Yes, there is still a lot of work to do.

For them.

For us.

Bystander (A Poem)

You hear it and you see it.

You say nothing, do nothing.

The more you wear your silence,

the LOUDER it grows and grows.

Do you feel its HEAVINESS?

Do you GRIEVE your lost innocence?

Why do you look away?

Why do you sideline yourself?

Why do you not care?

Listen, can you hear?

I'm quiet now, too.

You killed me.

—\o/ tmr

Conclusion

3 Cold Hard Truths

Among the current assault victims in this "greatest" nation in the world are truth, facts, science, critical thinking. The way an individual or entity regards (or disregards) truth is a key indicator for EVERYTHING across ALL industries, across ALL disciplines. Where truth is absent or under assault reveals to us EVERYTHING.

Know truth.

Seek truth.

Our power is found in truth. We are sealed in truth. When minds grasp truth and appropriate it, a power is unleashed such that NO weapon that comes against truth-bearers will have the victory. Not in your home, not in your workplace, not in your community. When we possess and exude a confidence, they don't like that. When we prosper and stand together, they grow enraged. Truth doesn't discriminate. It's not trying to be liked. Truth just is.

Cold Hard Truth #1

No one earthly is coming to save us.

There. I said it.

There is yet to be the widespread outrage needed to end racial inequity and injustice that continue to plague our communities, our workplace, our world.

The year is 2020. A year that'll be forever known as the year of covid; of hundreds of thousands of covid deaths; of escalated racial violence; of Breonna Taylor's, Ahmaud Arbery's, and George Floyd's murders; of massive lay-offs and unemployment; of Central Park Karen; of anti-maskers; of countless hurricanes, wildfires, and other natural disasters; of blatant voter suppression; of murder hornets, etc.

No one is coming to save us.

Joe Biden and Kamala Harris are not saviors for the Black community.

In the natural, we are the ones we've been waiting for.

We can PUSH and PUSH and PUSH some more by

calling out anti-Black racism

fighting for what's right and not settling for what's easy

controlling our own narratives

speaking truth to power even at great risk

owning our truth even when it's unpopular

showing up as our authentic self in spite of the haters

> **Ericka S. Riggs** here, and I'm speaking. Master the YOU Game. Be-YOU-tiful...Seek solitude to hear clearly. Learn to climb trees, to see the forest! Laugh more than you cry! Check your ego...let go of the chip on your shoulders...and say goodbye to distractors! Be thankful! And never give up on building your Be-YOU-tiful spirit! Make God proud of YOU!

Cold Hard Truth #2

While the world is focused on defeating the 'Rona, we have to also stay focused on STAYING ALIVE IN ALL SPACES. The vaccine for the 'Rona will arrive long before the one for racism.

Because we are subject to censure, silence, termination, intimidation, arrest, lynching...please, sisters, stay vigilant and have a plan for you and your loved ones during these times we find ourselves in.

Past is prologue. We have witnessed so much just this year alone causing our parents and grandparents to compare this dark period to the racial persecution of their day.

So please be mindful of the following threats:

OFF THE PLANTATION
being outside of designated spaces and entering white spaces (physical spaces, intellectual spaces, etc.)

REPORTING OF RUNAWAYS
also known as "the Karen" or "white caller crime" whereby random white people who can't mind their own damn bizness experience a visceral reaction to us and call 911

COMMANDS TO PRODUCE OUR PASS OR FREEDOM PAPERS
tangible proof that we belong in a white space (driver's license, membership card, resident pass, community pool pass, community fitness center pass, boarding pass, etc.)

STOPS BY PATTYROLLERS
stops by the po-po for any reason that may escalate when we ask the reason for the stop, when we don't use the term "sir," or when we reach for our ID, etc.

LYNCHING
killing of Black bodies by white people via bullet or choke hold which results in keeping us in a constant state of terror and trauma

Cold Hard Truth #3

One of the reasons we're always fighting and always blaxhausted is because we've never been free in this country. It's a brutal truth pill to follow. Hear me out.

In 2020 we are still NOT free. Come on somebody! The sooner we let that sink in, the better equipped we'll be to fight even when we're tired in body and spirit.

We can all agree that freedom is the power or the right to act, speak, think, and live one's life without hindrance, without restraint, and without BEING SHOT. As long as anti-Black racism systems, practices, and sentiments are upheld, we remain bound and enslaved.

Just as pattyrollers evolved into police, just as slavery evolved into the prison free-labor system, so too have actual chains and shackles been replaced with exactly what we have today—complex and interconnected networks of laws, systems, and practices held together by white supremacy glue and enforced by whiteness worshippers.

So, one more time.

We are NOT free.

It's a mind-blowing truth.

And we won't secure real freedom by begging, pleading, and reasoning with our oppressors. In the words of Assata Shakur, "Nobody in the world, nobody in history, has ever gotten their freedom by appealing to the moral sense of the people who were oppressing them."

Ruth Elizabeth Chale Pepito here, and I'm speaking. Note to self. You want more from now on. More positivity; more learning; more reading; more supporting small business; more cheering for black queens; more calling people out; more speaking up. Stay away from LinkedIn for a bit if you need to. Stop watching the news if that helps. Take care. There is still a lot of work to do.

3 Uplifting and Inspiring Truths

Just as our ancestors collectively never gave up and never lost hope, we do the same. We know the outcome. They have their white-man-made laws to which they subscribe, and we have ours—the laws of reaping and sowing. The God I serve is a God of love *and* justice.

I honor and respect that not everyone subscribes to faith-based principles, and so consider this. No matter how we slice it, it amounts to the same thing.

God don't like ugly.

Karma.

Pay-back is a bitch.

What goes around comes around.

Time to pay the piper.

A reckoning is coming.

Uplifting and Inspiring Truth #1

We Black women may get weary. But we know how to summon up the ancestors whose power as a people made them impossible to crush. They passed down to us survival DNA. They even turned scraps from the pig into savory and seasoned morsels! My grandma sho nuf could put her foot in some chitlins', chile! That's what we do. We take what whiteness deems the worst and transform it into a new thang, our cultural best. Innovation born of oppression, struggle, and an intense will to survive is just another example of our brilliance, resourcefulness, and power.

Lord knows, though, that white folks with their whiteness have tried over and over again to crush Black folks with active and persistent hate.

Stay with me, and gimme another sec. I'ma 'bout to soon get to the uplifting and inspiring part.

242

We as Black women have been doing so much of the heavy-lifting in fighting for the rights of ALL people, and yet who besides us is really fighting for us? We remain on the bottom and are subject to unspeakable abuses. Brother Malcolm nailed it in describing us. Unfortunately, his words have proven historically accurate, contextually appropriate, and timeless.

The day will come when his words will be obsolete!

Consider all that our collective Queendom has done, can do, and will do!

> **Dr. Shindale Seale** here, and I'm Speaking. The truths I discover in my Black sisters betray the lies we've so long believed. Sisters, we are astounding, unmatched, and unrivaled. Let us walk in our Legacy.

Just recently we saved this country from 4 more years of the most blatantly evil and racist president and administration in this country's history. Like we always do, Black women showed up! And we've been known to show out, too, when necessary!

Stacey Abrams, Keisha Lance Bottoms, Aimee Allison, LaTosha Brown, and other Black women leaders showed the world that we are the Queens that we are!

We have made sacrifices so that each person might thrive. We have always done what we do without expecting a thank you. But damn, a thank you and more widespread public acknowledgement would be nice! And still, we say to the world, "You're welcome!

Cuz, yeah, we did damn good this time in voting this orange racist menace outta here! Black women mostly did that! And if he refuses to leave January 20, send in Black women to throw his shit out on the front lawn of the big house, burn that shit, and then walk away Angela Bassett style like in *How Stella Got Her Groove Back*! White folks like a bonfire, right?

Black. Women. Get. Shit. Done.

Period.

Uplifting and Inspiring Truth #2

Yes, we'll meet with willful ignorance and hate head-on.

We'll be questioned, and we'll question back.

We'll be challenged, and we'll challenge back.

We'll be silenced, and we'll speak up, speak out!

Stay the course, sisters, because we're striking a blow.

And that makes us

EFFECTIVE.

Lakesha Mathis here, and I'm speaking. We always rise. We always find a way. In fact, we are the way. We are the tone setters, atmosphere shifters. And when we are off, everything is off. Protect us. We are peace. Support us. Listen to us. We set the tone in the home, in the office, at the party and the rallies.

Uplifting and Inspiring Truth #3

Sistahs, as we reach the end of this conversation in different states of blaxhaustion, uplift, sadness, hope, numbness, and blessed assurance, please know this—

We may be tired, but we are not broken.

We press on though they oppress us.

We rise while they rage.

We come together though they seek to divide.

From our mothers, grandmothers, great-grandmothers and beyond, we possess a "make a way outa no way" spirit.

244

Conclusion

We hold power in our DNA.

You.

Me.

US.

STRONGER TOGETHER.

WE ARE.

Still I Rise (A Poem)

You may write me down in history
With your bitter, twisted lies,
You may trod me in the very dirt
But still, like dust, I'll rise.

Does my sassiness upset you?
Why are you beset with gloom?
'Cause I walk like I've got oil wells
Pumping in my living room.

Just like moons and like suns,
With the certainty of tides,
Just like hopes springing high,
Still I'll rise.

Did you want to see me broken?
Bowed head and lowered eyes?
Shoulders falling down like teardrops,
Weakened by my soulful cries?

Does my haughtiness offend you?
Don't you take it awful hard
'Cause I laugh like I've got gold mines
Diggin' in my own backyard.

You may shoot me with your words,
You may cut me with your eyes,
You may kill me with your hatefulness,
But still, like air, I'll rise.

Conclusion

Does my sexiness upset you?
Does it come as a surprise
That I dance like I've got diamonds
At the meeting of my thighs?

Out of the huts of history's shame
I rise
Up from a past that's rooted in pain
I rise
I'm a black ocean, leaping and wide,
Welling and swelling I bear in the tide.

Leaving behind nights of terror and fear
I rise
Into a daybreak that's wondrously clear
I rise
Bringing the gifts that my ancestors gave,
I am the dream and the hope of the slave.
I rise
I rise
I rise.

— Maya Angelou

Rise Up (A Song)

You're broken down and tired
Of living life on the merry-go-round
And you can't find the fighter
But I see it in you, so we gonna walk it out

Move mountains
We gonna walk it out
And move mountains

And I'll rise up
I'll rise like the day
I'll rise up
I'll rise unafraid
I'll rise up
And I'll do it a thousand times again

And I'll rise up
High like the waves
I'll rise up
In spite of the ache
I'll rise up
And I'll do it a thousands times again

For you
For you
For you
For you

When the silence isn't quiet
And it feels like it's getting hard to breathe
And I know you feel like dying
But I promise we'll take the world to its feet

Conclusion

Move mountains
Bring it to its feet
Move mountains

And I'll rise up
I'll rise like the day
I'll rise up
I'll rise unafraid
I'll rise up
And I'll do it a thousand times again

For you
For you
For you
For you

All we need, all we need is hope
And for that we have each other
And for that we have each other
We will rise
We will rise
We'll rise, oh, oh
We'll rise

I'll rise up
Rise like the day
I'll rise up
In spite of the ache
I will rise a thousands times again

And we'll rise up
Rise like the waves
We'll rise up

In spite of the ache
We'll rise up
And we'll do it a thousands times again

For you, oh, oh, oh, oh, oh
For you, oh, oh, oh, oh, oh
For you, oh, oh, oh, oh, oh
For you

—Andra Day

Yaaassss, sistahQueen Maya and sistahQueen Andra Day!
With a poem and a song on our lips and in our spirit, we got this.
All of this.
It's what I know to be true in my bones and in my spirit.
Still we rise…rise up…and soar.
AND WE STILL HERE.
Ain't a damn thing they can do about that.

Theresa M. Robinson here, and I've spoken.
And still, I wrote what I wrote.
Ain't a damn thing they can do about that either.

Oppression Dictionary

The usual duplicity of language and meaning sunk to a new low during 2020. Because yeah, hell yeah, racism is coded into the language. Language is yet another colonizing tool in the ongoing colonization of bodies and minds. (I've also dropped in a few terms that don't fit the over-riding pattern but are, nevertheless, good terms to know.)

American
a coded synonym for white people (nearly everyone else hyphenates)

blaxhaustion ™
the constant and accumulating stress of racism over one's lifetime that causes wear and tear on the physical body and on emotional and mental well-being

blaxploitation ™
erasure, co-opting, theft, or appropriation of thought leadership and ideas of Black folks without proper crediting or compensation

boy
a term of subjugation used intentionally by racist white men in authority to address Black men

bringing our authentic self to work
bringing only the parts of us that make white people feel comfortable

Candace
a sell-out Black woman who has traded her Blackness for proximity to whiteness and white acceptance (named for Candace Owens, a nationally recognized sell-out figure)

cognitive distance
rationalizing and reconciling the profit-driven hypocrisy of opening the economy and exposing people to the risk of contracting the 'Rona and dying

content collectors
those of any race who habitually steal the content of Black folks and position it as their own with the intent of establishing their credibility, growing their influence, and boosting their business

coronaviracism™
the convergence of the coronavirus and racism pandemics and the adverse impacts on us and other communities of color

culture fit
integration-ability to align with the white power dominant status quo

cyber racism
social media racist trolling and Zoom bombing of us and non-Black POC

diversity
increase in representation of white women

early settlers
colonizers

essential
the work, rather than the expendable workers themselves who have tremendous value and keep society running

essential workers
disposable workers, most of whom are not paid a livable wage for maintaining all the moving parts of society and who often work without sick leave or health benefits

fake ally
a white person who claims allyship but is only all talk-show optics with no commitment and no receipts

forefathers
plunderers, rapists, and murderers

fragility
visceral defensiveness and rage of white folks during conversations about race and against anyone who calls them on their racist speech or behavior

freedom
the privilege of white folks to disregard rules or laws when rules and laws present an inconvenience to them

good people and heroes of liberty
yelling armed white men storming a state building

heritage
this nation's genocidal and racist history

illegal voters
Black and Brown voters

illegal votes
votes cast by Black and Brown folks

injustice
"just us" (thank you, Richard Pryor)

investigation
time and process devoted to getting all the white lies straight

justice
legal maintenance of whiteness and white power dominance

Karen
a dangerous white woman who can't mind her own damn business and likes to weaponize her whiteness by requesting to speak to a manager or calling the police on us for stupid shit because she can

Ken
basically a Karen with a penis but with the added role of protecting and defending Karens

law and order
white control over objections to oppression

lawful and peaceful protest
a group of armed white men yelling, and intimidating unarmed folks, and who are known to storm state capitals

lynching
modern-day killings of Black bodies that are mostly bullets this time but also knees and choke holds

Manifest Destiny
"entitled" theft of land and the justified removal or slaughter of the land's rightful occupants

mental illness
gratuitous benefit-of-the-doubt diagnosis afforded to white male domestic terrorists

no-knock warrants
open season on legal invasions of Black homes

patriotic
upholding white supremacy

patriotic education
white-centric education

patriots
gun-wielding mediocre white men terrorizing lawful protestors

performative allyship
a fake ally turning the show into a profitable anti-racism or diversity & inclusion business, oftentimes with our stolen content and thought leadership

police
slave patrols 2.0 or pattyrollers 2.0

professional
white-approved or white-sanctioned workplace speech, etiquette, or conduct

protect and serve
coded obligation of police to maintain and uphold the white supremacy status quo

racial gaslighting
psychological manipulation that seeks to minimize instances of racism and belittle our feelings and responses to the racism we experience

rapists, thugs, gangbangers
Black and brown youth

rights
a perk of whiteness that grants white folks God-given claims and legal claims that supersede any analogous claims by non-white persons

riot
a group of unarmed Black folks peacefully protesting

settled land
invaded and decimated

sir
a term by which racist white men in authority demand to be addressed

sons of bitches
silent kneeling black athletes

tompromised™
Black folks who picked the white team over the Black team and won't hesitate to throw members of the Black team under the bus if it will help to get in good with the white team

unprofessional

Black authenticity—speech, behavior, hair, clothing, etc.—that shows up in white spaces

wanton endangerment

a slap on the wrist pass to kill Black bodies with impunity

We the People

white people

whiteness

not a physical trait but a social construct that assigns power, benefits, and advantages to those perceived to be white

white preservation system™ (WPS)

the internal programming of white folks responsible for their visceral reaction against anything or anyone that encroaches on their comfort or convenience (frequently referred to as fragility)

white privilege

unearned and unquestioned benefits, advantages, and hook-ups that white folks get at our expense

white supremacy

the contrived big-ass lie that white folks tell themselves and everybody else that they and all they think, say, do, and produce is superior

wild-oat sowers

white male youth

About the Author

Theresa M. Robinson is one of seven anti-racism educators of 2020 featured in Forbes. As the founder and president of Master Trainer TMR & Associates, a training consulting firm, Theresa is a "disruptive inclusionist" in the diversity, equity, and inclusion (DEI) space who has dedicated her career to providing insights and practical strategies for navigating life and career.

As an ATD Certified Master Trainer and outspoken advocate of over 25 years of experience, Theresa takes participants beyond unconscious bias with a transformational experience that is centered on challenging hearts and minds, centered on the necessary discomfort that precedes growth and change, and grounded in truth.

Through workshops and 1:1 coaching, Theresa has advised C-Suite leaders of Fortune 500 companies and has partnered with Big 4 accounting firms, non-profits, and the tech and hospitality industries to advance strategic anti-racism and DEI initiatives that create an environment of belonging for all. Based in Houston, TX, she is already working on her fifth book that focuses on parenting while Black.

Other Books by Author

The WarriHER's Playbook on Self-Advocacy and Well-Being

 A powerful resource for working **women** at all career stages and across all industries, and for **facilitators** and **leaders** who run workshops and meetings. Filled with introspective practical "battle plans," it also draws on the wisdom and experience of 10 warriHER co-authors.

This go-to guide for women is loaded with 50 "battle plans."

Overcoming Gender Inequity: Real, Raw, Unapologetic Stories, Tips & Strategies

 A powerful resource for **women** at all career stages and across all industries, for **male allies**, and for **facilitators and leaders** who run DEI meetings, workshops, and courses. Filled with stories, experiences, and advice from crazy brave, fiercely resilient, stereotype-busting, insanely courageous, relentlessly determined, wildly successful women.

Each collabHERator was encouraged to just say it like it is and how she feels it—the good, the bad, and the ugly—without apology. **Live Strong. Live true. Live YOU!**

O-Syndrome: When Work is 24/7 and You're Not

 Achieve **Work-Life Balance** with this tell-it-like-it-is, shake-you-up, get-you-grounded, ignite-your-fighting-spirit guide to overcoming O-Syndrome. If you're overworked, overstressed, overburdened, over committed, over-loaded, over-obligated, over-tired, over-whelmed, overextended, over scheduled, and just plain over it, you are very likely suffering from O-Syndrome—today's 24/7 workplace equivalent of the elephant in the room.

Connect with Author

Well-Being Catalyst & Disruptive Inclusionist /
Facilitator / Speaker / Coach / Author

To reach **Theresa M. Robinson,** regarding speaking
engagements, training facilitation, coaching, upcoming
workshops, or to read her articles and posts, please connect
with her
@

www.theresamrobinson.com

info@theresamrobinson.com

linkedin.com/in/theresamrobinson/

+1.346.800.2822

Keynote Speaking & Training Facilitation Topics include:
Anti-Racism
DEI
Well-Being
Work-Life Balance
Life Strategies for Women
Self-Advocacy
Team Building